Powhatan Indian Place Names in Tidewater Virginia

Martha W. McCartney
&
Helen C. Rountree

Copyright © 2017
Martha W. McCartney and Helen C. Rountree
All Rights Reserved.
No part of this publication may be reproduced
in any form or by any means, including electronic
reproduction or reproduction via the Internet,
except by permission of the publisher.

Published by Genealogical Publishing Company
Baltimore, Maryland
Library of Congress Catalogue Card Number 2017938212
ISBN 978-0-8063-2062-5

Made in the United States of America

CONTENTS

Introduction..i

References Cited...iii

Powhatan Indian Place Names..........................1

Index to Indian Place Names.........................113

Index to Indian People.................................129

INTRODUCTION

Anyone passing through Tidewater Virginia or using the region's historical records is certain to encounter place names whose origin lies in the Algonquian language. Sometimes, Indian place names were spelled more than one way within a single document or in two documents recorded the same day. It is important to remember that the men who served as clerks of court or scribes in the Secretary of the Colony's office, where the original copies of land patents were maintained, were attempting to record names whose sound was foreign to them. For instance, in 1651 when someone patented some land on what we know as Skimino Creek, the Secretary of the Colony noted that his acreage bordered Kemino Creek. In 1662 cartographer Anthony Langston called the same stream Muskiminoughk Creek, while simultaneously a clerk in the Secretary's office called it Skimino Creek.

Cartographers, like government officials, were inconsistent when attempting to spell Indian place names. Within the text that follows, the earliest dated rendering is cited whenever a mapmaker identified a waterway or locality by that name. For example, if cartographers Peter Jefferson and Robert Brooke labeled a stream a certain way in 1747, and one or more of their successors used the same spelling, only the 1747 map is cited.

Tidewater Virginia's rivers and their tributaries, with their numerous twists and turns, make it difficult to identify the location of an Indian place name with a great degree of specificity. Therefore, within the text that follows, the words "left" or "right" have been used to identify the northerly or southerly side of a stream on which a specific cultural or geographic feature is located. This means of expression has been used in accord with the convention that streams flow toward their mouth and the sea. Likewise, the terms "upstream" and "downstream" have been used to indicate whether a site or feature was upstream or downstream from a specific reference point. For example, Manga Kemoxon, an Indian town, was located on the *left side* of the Rappahannock River in King George County. It also was *downstream* from Port Conway.

Indian place names are gathered under a main heading, which consists of their modern equivalent or most common spelling. Beneath that main heading can be found variations in the place name's spelling, listed in chronological order. This allows researchers to see how names changed over time. Readers are encouraged to make abundant use of the index, as it provides ready access to the main headings under which individual place names are clustered.

Introduction

From time to time, Dr. Helen C. Rountree, Professor Emerita of Anthropology at Old Dominion University, as co-author, has provided ethnohistorical information about the native people and events associated with specific locations. Interested readers are invited to explore her seminal work, *Pocahontas's People: The Powhatan Indians of Virginia*. A more recent volume, *John Smith's Chesapeake Voyages, 1607-1609,* provides numerous insights into the native way of life and native habitat.

REFERENCES CITED

Abbreviations

ARBER: *Travels and Works of Captain John Smith, President of Virginia and Admiral of New England, 1580-1631.* Edward Arber, ed. 2 Vols. Edinburg: John Grant, 1910.

BAR: Barbour, Philip. *The Jamestown Voyages Under the First Charter.* 2 vols. Philip L. Barbour, ed. Cambridge: The Hakluyt Society, 1969.

BEV: Beverly, Robert II. *History of the Present State of Virginia (1705)*, L.B. Wright, ed. Chapel Hill: University of North Carolina Press, 2013.

CJS: Barbour, Philip, ed. *Travels and Works of Captain John Smith, President of Virginia and Admiral of New England, 1580–1631.* 3 vols. Chapel Hill: University of North Carolina, 1986.

CSP: Palmer, William P. *Calendar of Virginia State Papers.* 11 vols. New York: Kraus Reprint, 1968.

CO: Colonial Office Papers. The National Archives, Kew, England. Survey Reports and microfilms, Rockefeller Library, Colonial Williamsburg Foundation, Williamsburg, Virginia.

DSVA: Cocke, Charles F. *Parish Lines of the Diocese of Southern Virginia.* Richmond: Virginia State Library, 1967.

DVA: Cocke, Charles F. *Parish Lines of the Diocese of Virginia.* Richmond: Virginia State Library, 1967.

EJC McIlwaine, *Executive Journals of The Council Of Colonial Virginia.* 5 vols. Richmond: Virginia State Library, 1925-1945.

FOR: Force, Peter, comp. *Tracts and Other Papers, Relating to the Origin, Settlement and Progress of the Colonies in North America.* 4 vols. 1836. Repr. Gloucester, MA: Peter Smith, 1963.

HAILE: Haile, Edward W., ed. *Jamestown Narratives: Eyewitness Accounts of the Virginia Colony: The First Decade, 1607–1617.* Champlain, VA: Roundhouse, 1998.

HEN: Hening, William W., ed. *The Statutes at Large: Being a Collection of All the Laws of Virginia.* 13 vols. Richmond: Samuel Pleasants, 1809–1823; repr. Charlottesville: University Press of Virginia, 1969. Database and digital images. http://vagenweb.rootsweb.com/hening/ 2006

References Cited

JHB: McIlwaine, H. R. et al., eds. *Journals of the House of Burgesses, 1619– 1776.* 13 vols. Richmond: Virginia State Library, 1905–1915.

LED: John Lederer, *The Discoveries of John Lederer with Unpublished Letters by and about Lederer to Governor John Winthrop, Jr. and an Essay on the Indians of Lederer's Discoveries,* William P. Cumming, ed. Charlottesville: University Press of Virginia, 1958.

LEO: Leonard, Cynthia M., comp. *The General Assembly of Virginia, July 30, 1619–January 11, 1978, A Bicentennial Register of Members.* Richmond: Virginia State Library Board, 1978.

LEW: Lewis, Clifford M. and Alfred J. Loomie. *The Spanish Jesuit Mission, 1570-1572.* Chapel Hill: University of North Carolina Press, 1953.

MCGC: McIlwaine, H. R., ed. *Minutes of the Council and General Court of Colonial Virginia.* Richmond: The Library Board, 1924; repr. Richmond: Virginia State Library, 1979.

MEADE: Meade, Bishop William. *Old Churches, Ministers and Families of Virginia.* 2 vols. Baltimore: Genealogical Publishing Company, 1992.

NN: Northern Neck Grants. Virginia Land Office 1692-1862. Microfilm on file at Library of Virginia, Richmond, and Rockefeller Library, Colonial Williamsburg Foundation, Williamsburg, Virginia. Database and digital images. Library of Virginia. *http://ajax.lva.lib.va.us/*

PB: Virginia Land Office Patent Books 1619–1660. Microfilm on file at Library of Virginia, Richmond, and Rockefeller Library, Colonial Williamsburg Foundation, Williamsburg, Virginia. Database and digital images. Library of Virginia. http://ajax.lva.lib.va.us/

PP: Rountree, Helen C. *Pocahontas's People: The Powhatan Indians of Virginia.* Norman, Oklahoma: University of Oklahoma Press, 1989.

SAIN: Sainsbury, William Noel et al. *Calendar of State Papers, Colonial Series, America and the West Indies.* 22 vols. Vaduz: Kraus Reprint, 1964.

SPOT: Spotswood, Alexander. *The Official Letters of Alexander Spotswood, Lieutenant-Governor of the Colony of Virginia, 1710-1722.* 2 vols. New York: AMS Press, 1973.

TYLER: Tyler, Lyon G. *Narratives of Early Virginia.* New York: Barnes and Noble

VCR: Kingsbury, Susan M., ed. *Records of the Virginia Company of London.* 4 vols. Washington: Government Printing Office, 1906–1935.

References Cited

Manuscripts and Miscellaneous Published Sources

Bassett Family Papers, 1650-1811. October 20, 1668, deed, Robert Abrahall to William Bassett, plat and courses of land, Romancoke in King William County, Mss2 B294 8b. Virginia Historical Society, Richmond, Virginia.

Black, William. February 24, 1774, letter to Bartholomew Dandridge. Mss1 L51 b8. Virginia Historical Society, Richmond, Virginia.

Bruce, Philip A., ed. "Public Officers in Virginia, 1702, 1714." *Virginia Magazine of History and Biography* 1 (1894):361-377.

Bruce, Philip A., ed. "Boundary Line Proceedings, 1710." *Virginia Magazine of History and Biography* 4 (1896-1897):30-42.

Byrd, William et al. William Byrd's Title Book, 1637-1743. Virginia Historical Society, Richmond, Virginia.

Byrd, William. *The Correspondence of the Three William Byrds of Westover, 1684-1776*, Marion Tinling, ed. Charlottesville: University Press of Virginia, 1977.

Chamberlayne, Charles G. *The Vestry Book and Register of Bristol Parish, Virginia, 1720-1789*. Richmond: Privately published, 1898.

Ferrar Papers, 1590–1790. Pepys Library, Magdalen College, Cambridge University, Cambridge, England. Microfilms, Rockefeller Library, Colonial Williamsburg Foundation, Williamsburg, Virginia.

General Assembly. *Acts and Joint Resolutions of the General Assembly of the State of Virginia, 1940 Session*. Richmond: Commonwealth of Virginia, 1940.

Lee Family Manuscripts 1638-1837. Mss 1 L51 f206-214. Virginia Historical Society, Richmond, Virginia.

Pargellis, Stanley, ed. "An Account of the Indians in Virginia." *William and Mary Quarterly* (Third Series) 16 (1959):228-243.

Percy, George. A Trewe Relacyon. *Tyler's Quarterly* 3 (1921):259-282.

Pindavako, Indian treaty between Pindavaco, the protector of the young king of Chiskyacke and representatives of Edward Wyatt, October 29, 1655. Brock Box 256 f 1. Huntington Library, San Marino, California.

References Cited

Robinson Family Manuscripts 1684-1798. 2 vols. Colonial Williamsburg Foundation, Williamsburg, Virginia.

Stanard, William G., ed. "Indians of Southern Virginia, 1650-1711: Depositions in the Virginia and North Carolina Boundary Case." *Virginia Magazine of History and Biography* 7 (1899-1900):337-351.

_____. "Indians of Southern Virginia, 1650-1711: Depositions in the Virginia and North Carolina Boundary Case, [conclusion]." *Virginia Magazine of History and Biography* 8 (1900-1901):1-11.

_____. "Virginia in 1677." *Virginia Magazine of History and Biography* 22 (1914):355-367.

Story, Thomas. *The Journal of the Life of Thomas Story.* Newcastle Upon Tyne: Isaac Thompson, printer, 1747.

Note: whenever original county court records have been used, references to specific record books have been provided.

Cartographic Works

Anonymous. "A New Map of Virginia, Maryland, and the Improved Parts of Pennsylvania and New Jersey," 1695. Colonial Williamsburg Foundation, Williamsburg, Virginia.

_____. "A New and Accurate Chart of the Bay of Chesapeake," 1776. Virginia Department of Historic Resources, Richmond, Virginia.

_____. "Eastern Half of Henrico County," [1878]. Virginia Department of Historic Resources, Richmond, Virginia.

Bache, A. D. "Part of Ingrams Bay, Dividing Creek and Fleets Bay," 1850. Virginia Department of Historic Resources, Richmond, Virginia.

_____. "Mouth of Rappahannock River," 1851-1856. Virginia Department of Historic Resources, Richmond, Virginia.

_____. "From Wolf Trap to Piankatank River," 1853a. Virginia Department of Historic Resources, Richmond, Virginia.

_____. "New Point Comfort to Wolf Trap," 1853b. Virginia Department of Historic Resources, Richmond, Virginia.

References Cited

_____. "Black [Back] and Pocosin Rivers, Chesapeake Bay," 1853-1854. Virginia Department of Historic Resources, Richmond, Virginia.

_____. "Rappahannock River from Holland Point to Brick Quarter," 1854. Virginia Department of Historic Resources, Richmond, Virginia.

_____. "Rappahannock River from Accaceek Point to Layton," 1855a. Virginia Department of Historic Resources, Richmond, Virginia.

_____. "Rappahannock River from Ferry Marsh to Accaceek Point," 1855b. Virginia Department of Historic Resources, Richmond, Virginia.

_____. "Rappahannock River from Layton to Punch Bowl," 1855c. Virginia Department of Historic Resources, Richmond, Virginia.

_____. "Smith's Point, Great and Little Wicomico Rivers," 1856. Virginia Department of Historic Resources, Richmond, Virginia.

_____. "Map of the Rappahannock River from Bailey's Bluff to Meachum's Creek," 1857a. Virginia Department of Historic Resources, Richmond, Virginia.

_____. "York River from Wormeleys Creek to Claybank," 1857b. Virginia Department of Historic Resources, Richmond, Virginia.

_____. "Map of Corrotoman River," 1857c. Virginia Department of Historic Resources, Richmond, Virginia.

_____. "York River from Clay Bank to Mount Folly," 1857-1858. Virginia Department of Historic Resources, Richmond, Virginia.

_____. "Map of Part of Accomac County," 1862a. Virginia Department of Historic Resources, Richmond, Virginia.

_____. "Chesapeake Bay," 1862b. Virginia Department of Historic Resources, Richmond, Virginia.

_____. "Coast of North Carolina and Virginia," 1862c. Virginia Department of Historic Resources, Richmond, Virginia.

Boye, Herman. "Map of the State of Virginia," 1826. Virginia Department of Historic Resources, Richmond, Virginia.

Braun, William. "Fairfields District, Northumberland County," 1885. Virginia Department of Historic Resources, Richmond, Virginia.

References Cited

Braden, Boyd. "Sketch Map of King George County," 185[ ]. National Archives, College Park, Maryland.

Captaine, Major Michael. "Carte de la Campagne en Virginie,"1781. Virginia Department of Historic Resources, Richmond, Virginia.

Churton, William. "The Line between Virginia and North Carolina," 1749. Virginia Department of Historic Resources, Richmond, Virginia.

Department of Commerce and Labor (D of C), Coast and Geodetic Survey, "Middle Part of Chincoteague Bay and the Ocean Beach," 1908. www.eshore.iath.virginia.edu/viewmaps.

Donn, J. W. "James River: Burwells Bay to College Creek," 1873. Virginia Department of Historic Resources, Richmond, Virginia.

Farrer, Virginia. "A Map of Virginia discovered to ye Hills," 1651. Colonial Williamsburg Foundation, Williamsburg, Virginia.

Fontaine, Lucy. "Survey of Barn Elms Tract in Middlesex County," 1828. Virginia Department of Historic Resources, Richmond, Virginia.

Franklin, Robert H. "Ware School District, Gloucester County," 1885a. Virginia Department of Historic Resources, Richmond, Virginia.

_____. "Petsworth School District, Gloucester County," 1885b. Virginia Department of Historic Resources, Richmond, Virginia.

Fry, Joshua and Peter Jefferson. "A Map of the Most Inhabited Part of Virginia," 1751-1775. Virginia Department of Historic Resources, Richmond, Virginia.

Gilmer, J. F. "Stafford County," 186[ ]. Virginia Department of Historic Resources, Richmond, Virginia.

_____. "Chesterfield County," 1863. Virginia Department of Historic Resources, Richmond, Virginia.

_____. "Caroline, Essex, King and Queen, and Essex Counties," 1864a. Virginia Department of Historic Resources, Richmond, Virginia.

_____. "King William County," 1864b. Virginia Department of Historic Resources, Richmond, Virginia.

_____. "Map of Prince George County," 1864c. Virginia Department of Historic Resources, Richmond, Virginia.

References Cited

Greene, William. "Map of the Peninsula," 1862. Virginia Department of Historic Resources, Richmond, Virginia.

Henry, John. "A New and Accurate Map of Virginia," 1770. Virginia Department of Historic Resources, Richmond, Virginia.

Herrman, Augustine. "Virginia and Maryland in 1670," 1673. Virginia Department of Historic Resources, Richmond, Virginia.

Hilgarde, J. E. "James River: Sandy Point to City Point," 1882a. Virginia Department of Historic Resources, Richmond, Virginia.

_____. "Lynn Harbor Bay and Vicinity," 1882b. Virginia Department of Historic Resources, Richmond, Virginia.

_____. "Lynn Harbor Bay and Vicinity," 1884. Virginia Department of Historic Resources, Richmond, Virginia.

Jenifer, Daniel. "[Map] for Sir Edmond Andros, All Accomack and All the Eastern Shore," 1693. Virginia Historical Society, Richmond, Virginia.

Jefferson, Peter and Robert Brooke. "Northern Neck of Virginia," 1736-1747. Virginia Department of Historic Resources, Richmond, Virginia.

Jefferson, Thomas. "A Map of the Country between Albemarle Sound and Lake Erie," 1787. Library of Virginia, Richmond, Virginia.

Keulen, Johannes Van. "Pars Kaert Van de Zee Kusten en Virginia," 1680-1696. New York Public Library, New York, New York.

Langston, Anthony. "Draft of York River in Virginia,"1662. Virginia Department of Historic Resources, Richmond, Virginia.

LaPrade, J. E. "Powhatan County," 1880. Virginia Department of Historic Resources, Richmond, Virginia.

_____. "Chesterfield County," 1888. Virginia Department of Historic Resources, Richmond, Virginia.

Madison, Bishop James. "Map of Virginia Formed from Actual Surveys," 1807. Library of Virginia, Richmond, Virginia.

Marzone, William. "Map and Profile of Experimental Survey of Norfolk Airline Railway," 1855. Virginia Department of Historic Resources, Richmond, Virginia.

References Cited

Mayo, William. "Northern Neck in Virginia," 1737. Colonial Williamsburg Foundation, Williamsburg, Virginia.

Moseley, Nannie L. "Hueguenot Magisterial District," 1885. Virginia Department of Historic Resources, Richmond, Virginia.

Ogilby, John. "Terrae Marie Nova et Virginiae Tabula," 1676. Virginia Department of Historic Resources, Richmond, Virginia.

Patterson, C. P. "Chickahominy River," 1873-1874. Virginia Department of Historic Resources, Richmond, Virginia.

Phelps, Lieutenant. "Reconnaissance of the Pamunkey and Mattapony Rivers," 1862. Virginia Department of Historic Resources, Richmond, Virginia.

Pierce, Benjamin. "Yeocomico River, Northwest, West, South Yeocomico Rivers," 1868. Virginia Department of Historic Resources, Richmond, Virginia.

_____. "James River, Virginia, Newport News to Pagan Creek," 1872. Virginia Department of Historic Resources, Richmond, Virginia.

Seib, John. "York River from Mount Folly to West Point," 1858. Virginia Department of Historic Resources, Richmond, Virginia.

Smith, John. "Virginia Discovered and Discribed [sic]," 1612. Virginia Department of Historic Resources, Richmond, Virginia.

Tatham, William. "Eastern Virginia and North Carolina," 1813. Virginia Department of Historic Resources, Richmond, Virginia.

Thornton, John. "A Map of Virginia, Maryland, Pennsylvania, New Jersey, Part of New York, and Carolina," 1698-1705.

Tyndall, Robert. "Robert Tyndall's Draughte of Virginia 1608," 1608. Virginia Department of Historic Resources, Richmond, Virginia.

United States Coast Survey (USCS). "Wallops and Assawoman," 1851. www.eshore.iath.virginia.edu/viewmaps.

_____. "Chincoteague Bay Topography,"1858. www.eshore.iath.virginia.edu/viewmaps.

United States Department of Agriculture (USDA). "Northampton County Sheet," 1917. www.eshore.iath.virginia.edu/viewmaps.

References Cited

United States Geological Survey (USGS). Topographic quadrangle sheets, . Library of Congress, Washington, D. C.

Velasco, Don Alonso de. [Untitled map], 1610. Virginia Department of Historic Resources, Richmond, Virginia.

Vingboons, Johannes. [Untitled map of Atlantic seacoast from Chesapeake Bay to Florida], 1639. Virginia Department of Historic Resources, Richmond, Virginia.

Warner, John. "A survey of the Northern Neck in Virginia as surveyed in the years 1736-1737," 1736-1737. Library of Congress, Washington, D. C.

White, John. [Untitled map of the East Coast from Virginia to Florida], 1585. Virginia Department of Historic Resources, Richmond, Virginia.

Wood, John. "Dinwiddie County," 1820a. Library of Virginia, Richmond, Virginia.

_____. "Chesterfield County," 1820b. Virginia Department of Historic Resources, Richmond, Virginia.

Zuniga, Pedro de. [Untitled chart of eastern Virginia], 1608. Virginia Department of Historic Resources, Richmond, Virginia.

Powhatan Indian Place Names in Tidewater Virginia

ACCOKEEK

Creek: Stafford County; a tributary on the left side of Potomac Creek, itself a tributary on the Potomac River's right side.

Aquokeeke (PB 6:299) (1669)
Ackhakeek (Madison map) (1807)
Accakeek (Boye map) (1826)
Accaceek (Bache map) (1855a)

Indian Town: Stafford County.

Accoqueck (Velasco map) (1610)

Place: Stafford County, at the head of Potomac Creek.

Ackokeek (Old Rappahannock County Record Book 1656-1664:351) (1665)
Akokeek (Stafford County Record Book 1686-1693:177a) (1690)
Okakeck (Fry-Jefferson map) (1751)

Point: Richmond County; on the left bank of the Rappahannock River; upstream from the mouth of Totuskey Creek.

Acokeck (Jefferson-Brooke map) (1747)
Accokick (Fry-Jefferson map) (1751)
Accochick (Anonymous map) (1776)
Accaceek (Bache map) (1855b)

ACCOMACK

County: established in 1634, encompassed all of Virginia's Eastern Shore; renamed Northampton County in 1643; Accomak County formed from the northern part of Northampton County in 1663; spelling changed to Accomack in 1940.

Acchawmacke (Northampton County Orders, Wills, Deeds &c 1632-1640:8) (1633)
Accawmack (HEN I:224) (1634)
Achommack (HEN I:249) (1643)
Accomak (HEN II:196-197) (1663)
Ackomack (Middlesex County Order Book 1673-1680:2) (1673)
Accomac (LEO 122) (1776)
Accomack (General Assembly) (1940)

Creek: Northampton County, a tributary of the Chesapeake Bay; now known as Cherrystone Creek

Accomacke (PB 5:400) (1664)
Accomack (PB 6:495 (1673)

Indian Town: Northampton County; on the left side of Old Plantation Creek; a king's house. In the 1620s and 1630s, their chief Esmy Shichans (whom the English dubbed the Laughing King) was the paramount chief of the Virginia Eastern Shore (PP 71-72, 81, 124).

Comokee (de Bry map) (1590)
Accowmack (Smith map) (1612)
Accomack (CJS II:150) (1612)
Accawmack (CJS II:164) (1612)
Acawmacke (CJS II:224) (1612)
Acomack (CJS III:288) (1624)
Accomacke (PB 1:49) (1626)
Accawmacke (HEN I:141) (1629)
Accowmac (Vingboon map) (1639)
Achomack (HEN I:293) (1645)
Ackomack (PB 3:269) (1653)
Accewmack (Ogilby map) (1676)

Indian Town: Northampton County; located immediately to the east of Eastville, on the right bank of Indian Town Creek; in December 1640 a 1,500 acre patent was given to the Accomac Indians as a preserve or reservation.

Powhatan Indian Place Names in Tidewater Virginia

After moving there, the Accomacs became known as the Gingaskins.

Accomac (MCGC 478)

Parish: Northampton County; formed by 1623 and encompassed Virginia's Eastern Shore; became Northampton Parish in 1643; renamed Accomack Parish in 1663 (DSVA 187, 190, 196).

Place: the Powhatan Indian name for Virginia's Eastern Shore.

Accawmacke (HEN I:141) (1629)
Acchawmack (Northampton County Orders, Wills, Deeds No. 1 1632-1640:78 (1636)
Accamacke (Northampton County Orders, Wills, Deeds No. 1 1632-1640:200 (1639)

ACCONOC

Indian Town: New Kent County; on the right bank of the Pamunkey River; located on the east side of the upper reaches of Hill Marsh, south of a nameless tributary.

Acconoc (Smith map) (1612)

ACCOQUECK

Indian Town: Caroline County, on the right bank of the Rappahannock River near Hollywood Bar and the present settlement of Olney Corner.

Accoqueck (Smith map) (1612)

ACCOSUMWINCK

Indian Town: King William County; on the left bank of the Pamunkey River; on the downstream side of Cohoke Mill Creek's mouth; a possible forerunner of Asiskewinck, Totopotomoy's fort.

Osamkateck (Zuniga map) (1608)
Accosumwinck (Smith map) (1612)
Asiskewincke (PB 3:16) (1653)
As-sas-kew-ing (PB 9:350) (1701)

ACCOTINK

Bay and Creek: Fairfax County; a tributary on the right side of the Potomac River; flows into modern Gunston Cove.

Accotynk (PB 6:633) (1677)
Oquatinck Creek: (Stafford County Record Book 1686-1693:29) (1686)
Accotinck (Stafford County Record Book 1686-1693:20-21) (1686)
Accotinck (Jefferson-Brooke map) (1747)

ACOUGHTANK

Indian Town: somewhere near the falls of the Potomac River, on the Maryland side.

Acoughtank (Velasco map) (1610)

ASQUACK

Indian Town: Richmond County; on the Rappahannock River's left side; short distance northeast of Cat Point Creek.

Asquack (Smith map) (1612)
Atquacke (CJS III:316) (1624)

ACQUINTON

Creek and Swamp: King William County; a tributary of Jack's Creek, a stream that is a tributary of the

Powhatan Indian Place Names in Tidewater Virginia

Pamunkey River's left side.

Quinton (Fry-Jefferson map) (1751)
Acquinton (Boye map) (1826)

Parish Church: the upper or westernmost church of St. John's Parish; the Acquinton Church was built around 1734, and is now in ruins.

ACQUASCA

Neck: Northampton County; on the left side of Old Plantation Creek; now nameless.

Aqusca (PB 3:289) (1654)
Acquasca (PB 4:538) (1662)
Aquasta (PB 7:196) (1682)

AJACAN

Place: Virginia Algonquian name for Virginia and adjacent regions, recorded by the 16th century Spanish.

Ajacan (de Bry 1590)

AMACOENCOCK

Indian Town: King and Queen County; on the left bank of the Mattaponi River, near Walkerton; identity uncertain.

Amacauncock (Zuniga map) (1608)

AMBURROCOMICO

Creek and Branch: Accomack County; on the seaside; by 1663, known as Gargaphie (now Gargatha) Creek.

Amburrocomico (PB 4:91) (1663)
Amburcomico (PB 4:92) (1663)

ANASKENOANS

Indian Town: Caroline County; on right bank of the Rappahannock River, west of Skinkers Neck and across the river from Corbins Neck.

Anaskenoans (Smith map) (1612).

ANCHANACHUCK

Place: Powhatan name for the people and country above the falls of the James River.

Anchanachuck (CJS I:55) (1608)

ANTOMMCASEWORD

Creek: Caroline County; now called Goldenvale Creek; right side of the Rappahannock River, across from Port Conway and the site of the Mangocommumkson Indian town.

Antommcaseword (Old Rappahannock County Deed Book 1656-1664:357) (1665)

APANAOCK

Indian Town: New Kent or Charles City County; on the Chickahominy River; between the Indian towns known as Mansa (at Old Neck) and Werawahone (near Chickahominy Haven).

Apanaock (CJS I:41) (1608)

APASUS

Indian Town: City of Portsmouth; became known as Craney Island, now much expanded by land-filling; possibly a Chesapeake tribal settlement unknown

Powhatan Indian Place Names in Tidewater Virginia

to the Jamestown colonists.

Apasus (de Bry map) (1590)

APOSTOQUO

Creek and Swamp: King and Queen County; probably Grass Creek, a tributary on the Mattaponi River's left side; ancient Indian ferry in the vicinity.

Apostique (PB 3:193) (1653)
Apostoquo (PB 3:225 (1653)
Apostiquo (PB 4:22) (1655)
Apotosque (PB 5:283) (1662)
Apostecoake (PB 6:101 (1667)
Apastenock (PB 6:188) (1668)
Apostecoque (PB 6:651) (1678)
Apostiquick (PB 7:525) (1686)
Apostequick Swamp (PB 9:707) (1705)
Pastcook (Fry-Jefferson map) (1751)

APPOCANT

Indian Town: New Kent County, a tributary on the Chickahominy River's left side, near Toe Ink Swamp.

Apocant (CJS I:45) (1608)
Appocant (Smith map) (1612)

APPOMATTOX

Bay: Chesterfield County; at the mouth of the Appomattox River.

Appomatock (PB 2:27) (1645)
Appamattock (PB 2:219) (1650)

Creek: Westmoreland County; a tributary on the Potomac River's right side; just upstream from Bridges Creek; known as Mattox after 1747.
Apamatuck (PB 4:129) (1657)
Appamattucks (PB 4:239) (1658)
Appomaticks (Northampton County Deeds, Wills, Etc. 1657-1666:100) (1661)
Appamattox (PB 5:168) (1662)
Appamattock (PB 5:290) (1662)
Appomattock (PB 4:113) (1664)
Mattox (Westmoreland County, Deeds and Wills 1:232) (1664)
Appatamocks (PB 6:1) (1666)
Appomattox (PB 6:56) (1667)
Apomatickes (PB 6:93) (1667)
Appamatricx (Herrman map) (1670)
Appamattocke (PB 6:691) (1679)
Appamattax (PB 7:181) (1682)
Apamatrix (Essex County Deeds and Wills 1692-1695:50-51) (1692)
Mattox (Jefferson Brooke map) (1747)
Mattex (Fry-Jefferson map) (1751)
Mattox (Tatham map) (1813)

Indian Town (Old): Chesterfield (formerly Henrico) County; on the left bank of the Appomattox River, above Swift Creek; abandoned by 1652; a king's house. Although the name of the chief in 1607 was not recorded, his sister, Opussonoquonuske, ruled a satellite town for him; in 1680, the chief was Peracuta (PP 10 et passim, 100, 109).

Apamatecoh (HAILE 117) (1607)
Apumatec (HAILE 112) (1607)
Apamatica (HAILE 93) (1608)
Apamatuc (CJS I:54) (1608)
Apamatuck (CJS I:31) (1608)
Mutticu "Quene of" (Tyndall map) (1608)
Appamatuck (Velasco map) (1610)
Apoamatake (HAILE 511) (1612)
Appamatuck (CJS II:146) (1612)
Appamatuke (CJS II:173) (1612)
Appamattock (PB 1:525 (1634)
Appamatuck (Vingboon map) (1639)

Powhatan Indian Place Names in Tidewater Virginia

Indian Town (New): Chesterfield (formerly Henrico) County; on the left bank of the Appomattox River; above Swift Creek and the site of the old town; established after 1634 but before 1652.

Appamattucke (PB 1:835 (1642)
Appamattox (PB 3:23) (1652)
Appomattux (HEN 2:274) (1669)
Appomatuck (HEN 3:85) (1691)

Indian Town: Westmoreland County; at the head of Mattox Creek.

Apamatockes (PB 4:41) (1656)
Apamuttucks (PB 4:239) (1658)
Appomattock (PB 5:354) (1662)
Appomatux (HEN II: 275) (1669)
Appomatuck (Ogilby map) (1676)

Indian Town: Richmond County; on the left bank of the Rappahannock River; between the Tapohanock Indian Town, on the right bank of Little Carter Creek, and the Nantaugstacum (Nantaughtacund) Indian town, north of Little Carter Creek's mouth.

Appamatuck (CJS I:53) (1608)

Parish: western Westmoreland County; formed from Nomini Parish around 1653-1654; named for Appomattox Creek; the parish became extinct in 1664 (DVA 166-167).

River: forms the boundary separating Chesterfield and Prince George Counties; a tributary on the James River's right side.

Apamatuck (CJS I:146) (1612)
Appamatuck (HAILE 603) (1612)
Appamattuck (PB 1:280) (1635)
Appamuttuck (PB 1:301) (1635)

Appamattucks (PB 1:336) (1636)
Appomattuck (PB 1:353 (1636)
Appamattock (PB 1:355) (1636)
Apamattuck (PB 1:469) (1637)
Appamattucke (PB 1:579) (1638)
Apamuttuck (PB 1:689) (1639)
Appamattocks (PB 1:767) (1641)
Appamattocke (PB 1:839) (1642)
Appomattocke (HEN I:315) (1646)
Appamattox (PB 3:23) (1652)
Appamattux (PB 3:41) (1652)
Appamatocke (PB 5:242) (1652)
Appamatocks (PB 5:224) (1663)
Appamatock (PB 5:324) (1663)
Appomattox (PB 5:350) (1663)
Appamatticx (Herrman map) 1670)
Appomatock (PB 6:447) (1673)
Hapomatucke (PB 7:216) (1682)
Appamatok (PB 7:535 (1686)
Happamatuck (PB 8:31) (1690)
Appomattock (Fry-Jefferson map) (1751)
Appomattock (Henry map) (1770)
Apomatok (Captaine map) (1781)
Appomattox (Bache map) (1853a)

AQUAKICK

Indian Town: on the Potomac River in Maryland; used as a reference point in a Virginia patent, which states that it was opposite "that part of Annocoston Indian Towne called Aquakick."

Aquakick (PB 6:73) (1669)

AQUATT

Place: Appalachian foothills.

Aquatt (LED 9) (1672)
Tanx-Paemotinck (LED 9) (1672)

AQUIA

Creek or River: Stafford County; a

Powhatan Indian Place Names in Tidewater Virginia

tributary on Potomac River's right side.
Quiyough (Smith map) (1612)
Oquiho (HAILE 606) (1612)
Ocquiah (PB 2:333) (1651)
Quiough (PB 3:134) (1652)
Quiriough (PB 3:192) (1653)
Oquioh (PB 3:302 (1654)
Oqui (PB 3:272) (1654)
Oquy (PB 3:284) (1654)
Oquio (PB 4:91) (1654)
Oquia (PB 4:310) (1654)
Oquiah (PB 4:38) (1656)
Oquina (PB 5:246) (1662)
Aquia (PB 5:364) 1662)
Quiough (PB 5:255) (1662)
Ochquayo (Herrman map) (1670)
Ocquia (PB 6:671) (1678)
Ochquayo (Anonymous map) (1695)
Acquia (Jefferson-Brooke map) (1747)
Acquia (Fry-Jefferson map) (1751)

Indian Town: Stafford County; on the west bank of the upper reaches of Aquia Creek.

Quiyough (Smith map) (1612)

Place: Virginia's Northern Neck.

AQUINTENOCCO

Creek and Swamp: King and Queen County; a tributary on the Mattaponi River's left side; west of the courthouse and now known as Courthouse Creek.

Quintenocke (PB 1934:282) (1653)
Aquintenocco (PB 4:48) (1656)
Aquintanio (PB 4:476) (1661)
Acquitimack (PB 5:283) (1662)
Aquintanocoe (PB 5:459) (1663)
Acquintenokes (PB 5:333) (1664)
Aquintenocko (PB 6:108) (1667)
Aquintinacok (Herrman map) (1670)
Aquintanocoke (PB 6:503) (1674)

Aquintinoco (PB 7:288) (1683)
Aquitanocke (PB 17:85) (85) (1691)
Aquintanocco (PB 9:610) (1704)
Aquintonocco (Fry-Jefferson map) (1751)
Anquemancock (Boye map) (1826)
Aquintenocco (Madison map) (1807)
Aqsummanook (Gilmer map) (1863)

ARMOGOTEGUE

Creek: King William County; tributary of the Mattaponi River's right side, near its junction with York River; in the vicinity of Port Richmond.

Annogotegue (PB 3:93) (1652)
Armogotegue (PB 3:93) (1652)

AROKOKE

Creek: Northampton County; a tributary of Nassawoddox Creek's left side; possibly present Warehouse Creek

Arakoko (PB 2:184) (1649)
Arokoke (PB 4:450) (1662)
Arrocoke (PB 6:372) (1671)
Arrakokes (PB 6:541) (1674)

ARRACAICO

Branch and Swamp: King and Queen County; a tributary on the Mattaponi River's left side; close to Goalders Creek.

Araykaco (PB 3:84) (1653)
Arracaico (PB 3:21) (1653)
Aracyaco (PB 3:326) (1654)
Arakeyaco (PB 3:355) (1655)
Arakiko (PB 3:340) (1655)
Arakaicoe (PB 4:237) (1658)
Arrakieco (PB 5:341) (1663)
Arrakeco (PB 5:345) (1663)

Powhatan Indian Place Names in Tidewater Virginia

Arrakico (PB 7:51) (1680)
Arrackico (PB 7:80) (1681)
Arracoicoe (PB 7:192) (1682)
Arrokieco (PB 7:271) (1683)
Arakeco (PB 7:271) (1683)
Arraicacoe (PB 7:617) (1687)
Arrakiako (PB 8:409) (1694)
Arricacioe (PB 9:96) (1697)
Arricacoe (PB 9:96) (1697)
Arracaco (PB 10:10) (1711)
Aracaico (PB 13:410) (1729)

ARRACOCK

Creek: Accomack County; a tributary of the Chesapeake Bay near Nandua Creek.

Arracock (PB 4:19) (1656)

ARRATICO

Creek: King and Queen County; a tributary on the Mattaponi River's left side; possibly Dixon Creek

Aratoco (PB 3:166) (1652)
Arratico (PB 5:193) (1655)

ARROHATTOCK

Creek: Henrico County; a tributary on the James River's left side; now a nameless creek upstream from Roundabout Creek.

Harrahattocks (PB 6:52) (1667)
Harahadocks (PB 7:633) (1687)
Harahadox (PB 7:633) (1687)

Indian Town: Henrico County; on the James River's left bank; approximately 2 ½ miles from falls; a king's house.

Arahatec (HAILE 115) (1607)

Arahatteak (Tyndall map) (1608)
Arssateck (Zuniga map) (1608)
Arsatecke (CJS I:29) (1608)
Arseteche (CJS I:31) (1608)
Arsahatecks (HAILE 556) (1611)
Arsahattacks (HAILE 555) (1611)
Arsahattocke (HAILE 822) (1611)
Arrohatack (HAILE 603) (1612)
Arohateck (HAILE 621) (1612)
Arrowhatock (CJS II:146) (1612)
Arrohatock (CJS II:147) (1612)
Arsahattock (CJS III:240) (1624)

Path: Henrico County; near the head of Four Mile Creek

Harrowhaddox (PB 6:279) (1669)

Place or Territory: Henrico County; on the James River's left bank, upstream from Farrar Island; site of the early seventeenth century European settlement known as the College.

Arahatecoh (BAR I:84) (1607)
Arsatyckes (HAILE 779) (1613)
Arrowhattocks (PB 1:155) (1634)
Arroehattocks (PB 1:326) (1635)
Harrow Attocks (PB 1:351) (1635)
Harroe Attocks (PB 1:403) (1636)
Harihatoxs (PB 1:451) (1637)
Arro Attocks (PB 1:553) (1638)
Arrohatuk (Vingboons map) (1639)
Harrahadocks (PB 3:11) (1653)
Harrahatocks (PB 5:236) (1662)
Harristocks (PB 5:164) (1665)
Harrahadockes (PB 6:52) (1667)
Arohateck (Ogilby map) (1676)
Harahadocks (PB 7:633) (1687)
Harahadox (PB 7:633) (1687)
Arrahattock (Fry-Jefferson map) (1751)
Arrahattock (Captaine map) (1781)

Powhatan Indian Place Names in Tidewater Virginia

ARSANTANS

Creek and Swamp: King and Queen County; a tributary on the Mattaponi River's left side; now called Corbin Creek; Tastine Swamp, at the creek's head, may be a corruption of the Indian name.

Arsantans (PB 3:166) (1652)
Tarsantyan (PB 3:355) (1655)
Arsantane (PB 4:181 (1658)
Arsantano (PB 4:181) (1658)
Assiotams (PB 4:289) (1660)
Arasantons (PB 4:89) (1662)
Assatiam (PB 4:89) (1662)
Tassiotomp (PB 5:456) (1665)
Tassiatums (PB 5:502) (1666)
Tassantium (PB 6:508) (1674)
Tansantium (PB 6:606) (1679)
Assatiams (PB 7:76) (1681)
Tassatiams (PB 7:175) (1682)
Tassatiames (PB 8:42) (1690)
Assatiame (PB 8:42) (1690)
Assatians (PB 6:687) (1699)
Assetisins (PB 9:262) (1700)
Arsantians (PB 9:590) (1704)
Tarsantyan Creek (PB 9:590) (1704)

Meadow: King and Queen County; near the creek of same name.

Assatiams (PB 6:593) (1676)

ASKAKEP

Indian Town: New Kent County; probably in the upper reaches of Diascund Creek

Ascacap (CJS I:41) (1608)
Askakep (Smith map) (1612)

ASKECOCACK

Indian Town: King William County; on the right bank of the Pamunkey River just above Grimes Landing.

Askecocack (Zuniga map) (1608)

ASSAMOOSICK

Swamp: Isle of Wight and Surry Counties; tributary on the Nottoway River's left side.

Acamewsock (PB 9:334) (1701)
Aschemusack (PB 9:336) (1701)
Assamusock (PB 9:720) (1706)
Assamusock (PB 10:152) (1714)
Atsamoosock (PB 11:319) (1723)
Arsamoosock (PB 12:264) (1725)
Assamoosick (Bache map) (1862c)

ASSANAMAYUSCOCK

Branch, Creek, and Swamp: King and Queen County; a tributary on the Mattaponi River's left side; now Garnetts Creek and its tributaries.

Awhore Cock (PB 4:83) (1650)
Hoarcock (PB 4:188) (1658)
Horecock (PB 4:188) (1658)
Whorecock (PB 4:174) (1658)
Ahorecock (PB 4:250) (1658)
Assanamayuscock (PB 4:258) (1658)
Assacamanscocke (PB 6:426) (1658)
Whore Cock (PB 5:328) (1662)
Horecock (PB 5:459) (1663)
Assamanket (PB 6:367) (1667)
Ashiamanscott (PB 6:203) (1668)
Ashnawaymanscott (PB 6:245) (1669)
Ashunwaymanscott (PB 7:712) (1669)
Whore Cock (PB 6:300) (1670)
Hashwamankcott (PB 6:425) (1672)
Assawaymanscott (PB 6:468) (1673)

Powhatan Indian Place Names in Tidewater Virginia

Ashawaymankirth (PB 6:556) (1675)
Hashwamacikers (PB 6:560) (1675)
Assanamyuscock (PB 6:633) (1677)
Horocock (PB 6:674) (1679)
Hashwamackott (PB 7:96) (1681)
Howcock (PB 7:325) (1683)
Assaway Mansecock (PB 6:634) (1688)
Herocock (PB 8:139) (1691)
Asseway Mansecock (PB 9:8) (1695)
Ascomonsock (PB 9:518) (1703)
Askamancock (Fry-Jefferson map) (1751)
Askamancok (Captaine map) (1781)
Ascamancock (Madison map) (1807)
Anscamansock (Boye map) (1826)
Asomastacock (Gilmer map) (1864a)

ASSAOMECK

Indian Town: Fairfax County; on the west bank of Dogue Creek.

Assaomeck (Smith map) (1612)

ASSATEAGUE

Inlet: Accomack County; the waterway between Assateague Island and Wallops Island; formerly called Mattapany Inlet.

Assateeg (PB 7:269) (1683)
Assateteage (PB 7:537) (1683)
Assateag (PB 8:235) (1692)

Island: Accomack County; on the ocean side, north of Chicoteague Island; now the boundary line between Virginia and Maryland passes through Assateague Island.

Asseteag (PB 9:3) (1695)
Assateague (Boye map) (1826)
Assateague (Marzone map) (1855)

ASSAWOMAN

Creek: Accomack County; a tributary of the Atlantic Ocean through Assawoman Inlet.

Assawoman (Madison map) (1807)

Inlet: Accomack County; the waterway between Wallops Island (to the north) and Assawoman Island (to the south).

Assawomen (PB 7:195) (1682)
Assawoman (PB 7:269) (1683)
Assawemen (PB 7:295) (1683)
Assowomen (PB 7:537) (1683)

Island: Accomack County; between the inlet of same name (to the north) and Kegotank Bay (to the south).

Assawoman (Boye map) (1826)
Assawaman (Marzone map) (1855)

Place: Accomack County; land near the creek of same name.

Assawomen (PB 6:64) (1673)
Assawoman (Northampton County Wills, Deeds, etc. 1718-1725:171) (1723)

ASSESQUIN

Creek: Hanover County; a tributary on the Pamunkey River's the right side; now called Whiting Swamp.

Assesquin (Fry-Jefferson map) (1751)
Assesquin (Captaine map) (1781)
Assaquin (Madison map) (1807)

ASSUWESKA

Indian Town: King George County; on

Powhatan Indian Place Names in Tidewater Virginia

the Rappahannock River's left bank near the mouth of Millbank Creek; possibly the same location as Nanzattico.

Assuweska (Smith map) (1612)
Asasaticon (PB 4:10) (1655)
Ausaticon (PB 5:194) (1664)

ATTAMTUCK

Indian Town: New Kent County; a tributary on the Pamunkey's River's right bank near the head of Holt's Creek.

Arramtuck (Smith map) (1612)

ATTAMUSPINCKE

Indian Town: New Kent County; on the Chickahominy River's left bank below Toe Ink Swamp.

Attamuspincke (CJS I:41) (1608)
Vttamuspieack (Zuniga map) (1608)

ATTANOUGHKOMOUCK

Place: a Powhatan word for Virginia.

Attanoughkomouck: inscription on Pocahontas's portrait, engraved by Simon van de Pas ca. 1617.

ATTAPIN

Creek: boundary between Westmoreland and King George Counties; a tributary on the Potomac River's right side; now called Rosier Creek.

Attapin (PB 2:274) (1650)
Attopinn (PB 3:71) (1653)
Attopin (PB 5:159) (1664)
Tappin (PB 5:162) (1664)

Attopine (PB 5:275) (1664)
Atopian (PB 6:681) (1679)
Attopiner (Jefferson-Brooke) 1747)
Attoppan (Fry-Jefferson map) (1751)
Atoppan (Henry map) (1770)
Attopan (Anonymous map) (1776)
Attopan (Tatham map) (1813)
Atopnan (Madison map) (1807)

AUHOMESK

Indian Town: Richmond County; on the Rappahannock river's left bank, below the mouth of Farnham Creek.

Aubomesk (Smith map) (1612)

AUREUAPEUGH

Indian Town: Essex County; on the Rappahannock River's right bank; west of Green Bay and east of Portobacco Creek.

Aurenapeugh (Velasco map) (1610)
Aureuapeugh (Smith map) (1612)

BOCKATENOCK

Bay and Creek: Accomack County; flows into the Atlantic Ocean; possibly modern Greens Creek.

Bockatenock (PB 6:32) (1666)
Bockatnocktun (PB 6:34) (1666)
Place: Accomack County; near the bay of the same name; probably near modern Exmore.

Bockanoctun (PB 6:34) (1666)
Bockatenoctun (PB 6:35) (1666)

Powhatan Indian Place Names in Tidewater Virginia

CANTAUNKACK

Indian Town: Gloucester County; on the York River's left bank, between Carter and Aberdeen Creeks. In ca. 1610, Ononnamo was the chief here (HAILE 628).

Cantaunkack (Smith map) (1612)

CAPAHOSACK

Creek: York County; a tributary on the York River's right side; analogous to Carter's Creek, at Camp Peary.

Capahosack (Henry map) (1770)

CAPAHOSIC

Creek: Gloucester County; a tributary on the York River's left side; by 1826 known as Cedar or Cedarbush Creek.

Capahosack Creek (PB 8:194) (1691)
Capahosick (PB 10:123) (1713)

Indian Town: Gloucester County; on the York River's left bank, between Timberneck and Cedarbush Creeks; "given" to John Smith by Powhatan, 1608.
Capahowesick (Zuniga map) (1608)
Capahowasicke (CJS I:57) (1608)
Capahowasick (Velasco map) (1610)
Capahowasick (Smith map) (1612)
Capahawosick (CJS III:151) (1624)
Capahosak (Fry-Jefferson map) (1751)

Place: Gloucester County; on the York River's left bank, near the town of the same name.

Cappahossic (Bache map) (1857-1858)
Cappahousic (Franklin map) (1885b)

CASSAPECOCK

Indian Town: New Kent County; somewhere on the Pamunkey River's right bank; location very uncertain. In ca. 1610, the chief in this town was Keyghaughton (HAILE 628).

Cappapecock (HAILE 628) (1612)

CATTACHIPTICO

Indian Town: King William County; on Pamunkey River's left bank, on the upstream side of Moncuin (Manquin) Creek's mouth, and above Goddin's Island; identified as "the Indian Fort" on Anthony Langston's map (1662).

Cakkiptaco (Zuniga map) (1608)
Cattachipico (Velasco map) (1610)
Cattachiptico (Smith map) (1612)

CAWSUNKER

Swamp: Southampton (formerly Isle of Wight) County; somewhere on the left side of the Nottoway River.

Cawsunker (PB 11:319) (1723)

CAWUNKACK

Indian Town: New Kent County; on the Pamunkey River's right bank, opposite Sweet Hall Marsh and east of White Oak.

Cawunkack (Zuniga map) (1608)

CAWWONTOLL

Indian Town: Richmond County; on Rappahannock River's left bank;

Powhatan Indian Place Names in Tidewater Virginia

upstream from the mouth of Wilna Creek.

Cawwontoll (Smith map) (1612)

CECOCOMAKE

Indian Town: Prince George County; extension of the Weyanock territory south of the James River; probably a Weyanock Town situated inland, at the head of Powells Creek.

Cecocomake (HAILE 622) (1612)

CHACOMA

River: King George County; tributary on the Potomac River's right side; probably modern Upper Machodoc Creek.

Chacoma (Northumberland County Deeds and Orders 1650-1652:50) (1650)

CHAMOCKIN

Place: near the boundary between New Kent and Hanover Counties; on the Pamunkey River's right bank, between Matadequin and Black Creeks.

Cheemockin (PB 3:51) (1653)
Chomocken (PB 3:301) (1654)
Chimahocans (PB 4:54) (1656)
Chymahocans (PB 4:54) (1656)
Chamockin (PB 4:146) (1657)
Chemokins (PB 5:267) (1663)
Chamokins (PB 5:240) (1664)

Swamp: Hanover County; a tributary on the right side, being the first branch near the mouth, of Matadequin Creek, itself a tributary on the Pamunkey River's right side.

Chemokin (Hanover County Deed Book 1783-1792:151) (1787)

CHAPPAWAMSICK

Creek: part of the boundary between Stafford and Prince William Counties; a tributary on the Potomac River's right side; now spelled Chopawamsic.

Chepawomsick (Stafford County Record Book 1686-1693:10-10a) (1686)
Chepawonsick (Stafford County Record Book 1686-1693:7-7a) (1686)
Cappatsowsick (Mayo map) (1737)
Chappawamsick (Jefferson-Brooke map) (1747)
Chapawansick (Warner map) (1747)
Chopawamsick (Fry-Jefferson map) (1751)
Chopowansic (Henry map) (1770)
Chopawamsic (Boye map) (1826)

CHECHOBANKE

Indian Town: City of Newport News; on the James River's left side, facing Hampton Flats, near the Boat Harbor.

Chechobanke (Tyndall map) (1608)

CHECKTANCK

Creek: Northumberland County; a tributary on the Potomac River's right side; probably modern Hulls Creek.

Checktanck (Herrman map) (1670).

CHEKROES

Bay: James City County; on the Chickahominy River's left side, between Shields Point and Bush Neck.

Powhatan Indian Place Names in Tidewater Virginia

Chechqueroes (PB 1:562) (1638)

Branch: James City County; a tributary of Gordon's Creek, near its head.

Chekroes (Lee Family Papers Mss 1 L 51) (1714)

Creek: James City County; on the Chickahominy River's left side; now known as Gordon's Creek.

Checkeroes (PB 1:601) (1635)
Checkros (PB 1:430) (1637)
Checqueroes (PB 1:624) (1638)
Checroes (PB 1:684) (1639)
Checheroes (PB 1:868 (1642)
Chechqueroes (PB 1:868) (1642)
Chiskroes (PB 2:264) (1650)
Cherkrose (PB 3:31) (1652)
Chekroes (PB 3:263) (1654)
Chekerors (PB 5:398) (1665)
Checkarus (PB 6:201) (1668)
Checkerhouse (PB10:221) (1714)

Neck: James City County; on the Chickahominy River's left side; now known as Bush Neck.

Checquers (PB 1:328) (1635)
Checkroes (PB 1:363 (1635)
Checkeroes (PB 1:372) (1636)
Checroes (PB 1:724) (1641)
Chekoes (PB 3:263) (1654)

CHECOPISSOWO

Indian Town: Caroline County; on the Rappahannock River's right side, upstream from Goldenvale Creek.

Checopissowo (Smith map) (1612)

CHEPECO

Indian Town: somewhere on the Pamunkey or Mattaponi River; location very uncertain. The chief of this town in ca. 1610 was Opopohcumunk (HAILE 628).

Chepeco (HAILE 628) (1612)

CHERAKO

Ferry: Northumberland County; on the Potomac River's right side; in the vicinity of the Coan River.

Cherako (Northumberland County Order Book 1652-1665:399) (1664)

CHERITON

Creek: Northampton County; a tributary of the Chesapeake Bay; now known as Cherrystone Inlet.

Cheriton (Fry-Jefferson map) (1751)

CHESAKAWON

Indian Town: Lancaster County; on the Rappahannock River's left bank; near the head of Tabbs Creek.

Chesakawon (Smith map) (1612)

CHESAPEAKE

Bay: a tributary of the Atlantic Ocean into which flow Virginia's James, York, Rappahannock and Potomac Rivers.

Chesepiooc (de Bry map) (1590)
Chesseian (BAR I:82) (1607)
Chesupioc (BAR I:135) (1608)
Chissiapiacke (CJS I:27) (1608)

Powhatan Indian Place Names in Tidewater Virginia

Chesiapiack (CJS I:79) (1608)
Chesapeack (Smith map) (1612)
Chaesapheac (HAILE 740) (1612)
Chesepeiake (PB 1:49) (1626)
Chesepeyack (PB 1:86) (1628)
Chesopean (PB 1:179) (1635)
Chisopeian (PB 1:387) (1636)
Chesopeian (PB 1:663) (1639)
Chesapeack (Vingboons map) (1639)
Cheesopean (PB 1:770) (1641)
Chesipiacke (PB 1:799) (1642)
Chisopeiake (PB 1:865) (1642)
Cheesepiake (PB 4:67) (1642)
Chisapeyak (PB 2:262) (1650)
Chesepiake (PB 3:106) (1652)
Chesepeack (PB 4:19) (1656)
Chisapian (PB 5:216) (1662)
Chespiack (PB 5:190) (1663)
Chesapiake (PB 5:336) (1663)
Chesepaik (PB 6:81) (1667)
Chesepiack (PB 6:176) (1668)
Chisapeiacke (PB 6:42) (1672)
Chesipeacke (PB 6:637) (1678)
Cheespiack (PB 7:14) (1679)
Chesapeax (PB 7:114) (1681)
Chesapeac (PB 8:117) (1690)
Chesapeake (Bache map) (1856)

Creek: City of Chesapeake; near Lynnhaven Bay.

Chesapyan (Hilgarde map) (1884)

Indian Town: City of Chesapeake, somewhere along the Southern Branch of the Elizabeth River; located in an area impacted by extensive industrial development; a king's house.

Chesepiooc (White map) (1585)
Chessepians (HAILE 106) (1607)
Chysapeack (Zuniga map (1608)
Checepiock (Velasco map) (1610)
Chesapeack (Smith map) (1612)
Chisapeack (CJS III:178) (1624)
Chissapeack (CJS III:291) (1624)
Chisapeak (CJS III:319) (1624)
Chesapeeck (Ogilby map) (1676)

River: City of Virginia Beach; a tributary of the Chesapeake Bay; by 1635 known as Linhaven or Lynhaven River.

Chisapeack (CJS I:146) (1612)
Chisopeiacke (PB 1:381) (1630)
Chisopeian (PB 1:315) (1635)
Chesopeian (PB 1:327) (1635)

CHESCONNESSEX

Creek: Accomack County; a tributary of the Chesapeake Bay.
Chyconnessecks (PB 3:339) (1655)
Chiccanssecks (PB 4:2) (1655)
Chissenessecks (PB 4:21) (1656)
Chichonessecks (PB 4:22) (1656)
Chiccanessecks (PB 4:455) (1660)
Chucanessecks (PB 4:466) (1661)
Chichanesecks (PB 4:536) (1661)
Chechanesscks (PB 4:543 (1662)
Chingandokee (PB 4:540) (1662)
Chucanesseks (PB 5:185) (1664)
Chickanesseks (PB 6:176) (1668)
Chissenossick (Herrman map) (1670)
Chessanesson (Northampton County Orders, Wills 1674-1679:336) (1678)
Chickonessex (PB 10:181) (1714)
Chesscon (Boye map) 1826)
Chesconessex (Marzone map) (1855)

Indian Town: Accomack County; somewhere on Chesconnessex Creek. In the early 1660s, the chief of this tribe was Nochetrawen.
Chissenessecks (PB 4:21) (1656)
Checconessick (Accomack County, Deeds and Wills 1663-1666: 22) (1663)
Chicconesseck (Accomack County, Deeds and Wills 1663-1666:39) (1663)

Powhatan Indian Place Names in Tidewater Virginia

Chiccanessecks (Accomack County, Deeds and Wills 1663-1666: 53) (1663)
Chisonessex (Stanard, "Indians of Southern Virginia," 363) (1702)
Chiconessex (BEV 184) (1704)

Place: Northampton County; an English plantation.

Chiconessox (Northampton County Wills, Deeds, etc. 1711-1718:58) (1708)

CHESPAIACK

Path: King and Queen County; between the Mattaponi River and Dragon Swamp (which is the headwaters of the Piankatank River).

Chespaiack (PB 5:344) (1663)

CHESTUXEN

Creek: Essex County; on the Rappahannock River's right bank; southeast of Occupacia Creek; possibly Margaret Lee Swamp or Sluice Creek.

Chestucson (PB 6:436) (1672)
Chesstuxent (Essex County Deeds and Wills 1692-1695:387) (1692)
Chesstixent (Essex County Deeds and Wills 1695-1699:332) (1699)

Run: Richmond County; on the Rappahannock River's left side, near the mouth of Totuskey Creek and Accaceek Point.
Chestuxen (PB 5:301) (1663)

CHETECKCAURAH

Creek and Swamp: Sussex (formerly Prince George and Surry) County; on the Nottoway River's right side, near Harry Swamp. The name may not be Virginia Algonquian.

Cheteckcaurah (PB 9:740) (1706)
Chetecoraw Swamp (PB 10:449) (1719)

CHONAMUN

Branch: Richmond County; probably a branch of Totuskey Creek near Warsaw.
Chonamun (Richmond County Deed Book 2 [1693-1695]:162) (1696)

CHICAMUXEN

Place: Fairfax County; on the southwest bank of Little Hunting Creek, a tributary on the Potomac River's right side.

Chingomuxon (PB 4:141) (1657)
Chiccomoxen (Fry-Jefferson map) (1751)

CHICKACONE

Indian Town: Northumberland County; on the Coan River's right bank; a king's house. In the late 1650s, Machywap was this tribe's chief (PP 123).

Cekakawwon (Smith map) (1612)
Sekacawone (CJS II:148) (1612)
Cecocawone (CJS II:227) (1612)
Cecocawonee (CJS III:167) (1624)
Cekacawone (CJS III:304) (1624)
Chicacoen (FOR II:7:32) (1648)
Chichacone (PB 4:75) (1656)
Chickacone (PB 4:208) (1657)
Chikacone (PB 4:300) (1662)
Chiccacoane (PB 6:98) (1667)
Chicocoan (Herrman map) (1670)

Parish: Northumberland County; its territory extended in a westerly direction, to the west of Wiccocomico Island;

Powhatan Indian Place Names in Tidewater Virginia

established in 1645 and in 1664 became Fairfield Parish (DVA 162-163).

Chickacone (HEN I:352) (1646)

Path: Lancaster and Northumberland Counties; a trail leading from Chicacone town to the Morattico and Totuskey towns.

Chicacone (PB 3:131 (1652)
Chicokone (PB 3:73) (1653)
Chickacone (PB 4:296) (1661)
Chikacone (PB 5:202) (1662)
Chiccacone (PB 6:165) (1668)
Chichacone (PB 6:629) (1677)

Place: territory bordering the Potomac River's right side, on the west side of Hull Creek's mouth.

Chickcoun (HEN I:352) (1646)
Chickacone (PB 4:208) (1657)
Ceekacawone (Northumberland County Deed Book 25:50) (1827)
Cekacowone (Northumberland County Deed Book H:287) (1884)
Cikacawone (Northumberland County Deed Book H:430) (1885)

River: Northumberland County; a tributary on the Potomac River's right side.

Chicokolne (PB 2:185) (1649)
Chicocone (PB 2:275) (1650)
Chicacone (PB 3:131) (1652)
Checkakone (PB 3:134) (1652)
Chickacoan (PB 4:303) (1652)
Chickacone (PB 3:64) (1653)
Chicokoone (PB 3:227) (1654)
Chycokoon (PB 3:278) (1654)
Chicokone (PB 3:344) (1655)
Chickakone (PB 4:153) (1655)
Chichacone (PB 4:75) (1656)

Chickacoone (PB 5:289) (1662)
Chickocone (PB 6:11) (1666)
Chikacone (PB 5:511) (1664)
Coan (Fry-Jefferson map) (1751)

CHICKAHOMINY

Fort: New Kent County; high ground on the right side of Diascund Creek; site of an English-built fort also known as Fort James; built in 1645-1646 at the expense of Thomas Rolfe, Pocahontas's son, in exchange for 400 acres.

Chickahominy Fort (HEN I:327) (1646)

Fort: New Kent County; an Indian-built fort on the right side of the Pamunkey River.

Chickahominy Fort (PB 4:109) (1657)

Fort: King William County; an Indian-built fort attacked by the Senecas; on the Mattaponi River's right bank, probably between Aylett and Herring/Dorrell Creeks.

Chickahominy Fort (EJC I:53) (1683)

Gate: location in James City or New Kent County, on the Chickahominy River's left bank near Diascund Creek which forms part of the boundary between the two counties.

Chickahominy Gate (PB 5:303) (1663)

Indian Towns and Tribe: James City and Charles City Counties; villages located on both sides of the Chickahominy River.

Chechohomynaies (BAR 226) (1608)
Chikhamania (CJS I:39) (1608)

Powhatan Indian Place Names in Tidewater Virginia

Chikahamania (CJS I:39) (1608)
Chickahominy (CJS I:41) (1608)
Chickahamania (CJS I:71) (1608)
Chickahomaniens (CJS I:71) (1608)
Chickahamanian (CJS I:91) (1608)
Chicahamanya (CJS I:91) (1608)
Chickahamine (CJS II:211) (1612)
Chickahamina (CJS II:239) (1612)
Chickahamino (CJS II: 262) (1612)
Chicohamians (HAILE 509) (1612)
Chicohominie (HAILE 810) (1614)
Checkahomanies (HAILE 845) (1614)
Chicohominies (HAILE 846) (1614)
Chikahominy (HAILE 846) (1614)

Indian Town: in King William County; on the Mattaponi river's right bank, between the Aylett and Herring/Dorrell Creeks. In 1661, the councilor who represented the people to the English was a man named Harquip (HEN II: 39).

Chickahamania (Vingboons map) (1639)
Chichahominy (MCGC:361) (1649)
Chicahominy (EJC I:394) (1656)
Chickahomynies (HEN I:403) (1656)
Chichominyes (HEN I:468) (1658)
Chickahomini (HEN II:34) (1661)
Chikahomani (PB 5:412 (1663)
Chickahomonies (HEN II:275) (1669)
Shickehamany (LED 15) (1672)
Chickahominy (Story 162) (1698)

Indian Town: King and Queen County; on the Mattaponi River's left bank, facing Rickahock Bar.

Chickahominy (EJC I:320; CSP I:22) (1684)

Parish: Charles City and James City Counties; formed in 1632 and straddled the Chickahominy River; became extinct in 1643, when Wallingford Parish was formed (DSVA 195).

Ridge: New Kent County; high ground on the right side of Diascund Creek; site of an English-built fort known as Fort James or the Chickahominy fort, erected in 1645-1646.

Chiquohomine (HEN I: 293) (1646)

River: a tributary on the James River's left side; near its mouth it forms the boundary between Charles City and James City counties; in its upper reaches it forms the boundary between Charles City and New Kent counties.

Chickahominy (CJS I:41) (1608)
Chickahamania (Smith map) (1612)
Chichahominy (PB 1:137) (1632)
Chickahominy (PB 1:393) (1636)
Chikahomony (PB 2:361 (1643)
Cheychohominy (HEN I:287) (1644)
Chiquohomine (HEN I:293) (1645)
Chickahamonie (PB 2:96) (1646)
Chicohominey (PB 2:238) (1650)
Chicohominy (PB 2:271) (1650)
Chicahominy (PB 2:277) (1651)
Chicohamony (PB 2:329) (1651)
Chickohominy (PB 2:351) (1651)
Chicohamy (PB 2:321) (1651)
Chichamony (PB 3:245) (1653)
Chycohominy (PB 3:290) (1653)
Chychohominy (PB 3:263) (1654)
Chicihominy (PB 3:307) (1654)
Chicohomminy (PB 3:359) (1655)
Chichohominy (PB 4:18) (1655)
Chikahomany (PB 4: 312) (1662)
Chikahominy (PB 4:106) (1663)
Chickahomany (PB 5:349) (1663)
Chickahomeny (PB 5:358) (1663)
Chikahomani (PB 5:455) (1665)
Chicohomine (Herrman map) (1670)
Chickahamania (Ogilby map) (1676)
Chickahominy (Fry-Jefferson map) (1751)

Powhatan Indian Place Names in Tidewater Virginia

Swamp: boundary between Charles City and New Kent Counties; headwaters of the Chickahominy River.

Chicahominy (PB 4:105) (1657)
Chickahominy (PB 4:152) (1658)
Chickahomyny (PB 4:255) (1658)
Chikahomani (PB 4:325) (1662)
Chikahomany (PB 4:325) (1662)
Chickahomeny (PB 5:365) (1662)
Chickehominy (PB 5:332) (1663)
Chickhomeny (PB 5:278) (1663)
Chiccahomony (PB 6:96) (1667)

CHINCOTEAGUE

Bay: Accomack County, Virginia, and Worcester County, Maryland; east and north of Chincoteague Island.

Creek: Accomack County; a tributary of Chincoteague Bay.

Gingotege (PB 5:183) (1664)
Gintotege (PB 5:379) (1664)
Gingoteage (PB 5:495) (1666)
Gingoatege (PB 6:120) (1668)
Gingoeteage (PB 6:286) (1670)
Gingo Teage (PB 6:392) (1671)
Gingotake (PB 6:456) (1673)
Chincoteague (Marzone map) (1855)

Indian Town: Accomack County; probably near Chincoteague Creek; by 1705 the tribe had joined other Maryland Indians (BEV 182) (1704)

Gingo Teage (FOR III:10:46) (1649)
Gingateege (Northampton County, Deeds, Wills and Orders 3: 217) (1650)
Jingoteige (PB 6:607) (1675)
Gentgoteage (PB 6:615) (1677)
Gingoteag (PB 6:637) (1678)
Jengotege (Accomack County, Wills, Deeds And Orders 1678-1682:53) (1678)
Gingotege (Stanard, "Indians of Southern Virginia," 363) (1702)

Inlet: Accomack County; the inlet between a string of barrier islands; adjacent to Chincoteague Island and the Atlantic Ocean.

Island: Accomack County, Virginia; now spelled Chincoteague; borders the Atlantic Ocean; historical maps often place the island in Maryland.

Chingoteacq (Herrman map) (1670)
Gingoteage (PB 6:405) (1671)
Jengoteag (PB 6:421) (1672)
Chincoteag (PB 6:430) (1672)
Gingoteag (PB 6:430) (1672)
Gengoteage (PB 7:395 (1684)
Gingoteague (PB 8:110) (1690)
Jingoteague (PB 8:168) (1691)
Jengoteague (PB 8:235) (1692)
Jengotegue (PB 8:417) (1695)
Jingoteague (Northampton County Deeds, Wills, &c 19 [1708-1717]:23 (1707)
Jengoateague (Northampton County Deeds, Wills, &c 1711-1718:58) (1708)
Jengoteague (Northampton County Deeds, Wills, &c 1711-1718:58) (1708)
Jenckotage (Northampton County Deeds, Wills, &c 1718-1725:81) (1720)
Chingoteacq (Fry-Jefferson map) (1751)
Jingotegue (Northampton County Wills, & Inventories 1760-1762:398) (1761)
Chingateague (Jefferson map) (1787)
Chingoteague (Madison map) (1807)
Chincoteague (Boye map) (1826)

CHINGANDEHEE

Creek: Northampton County; a tributary of Nassawaddox Creek; possibly Church Creek.

Powhatan Indian Place Names in Tidewater Virginia

Chingandehee (PB 2:185) (1649)
Chingandokee (PB 4:540) (1662)

CHINGOGAN

Place: Northumberland County; a neck of land defined by Bridgeman Creek and Fountain Cove, tributaries of Presley Creek and Hull Creek; now known as Newman's Neck.

Chinckahan (Northumberland County Record Book 1652-1658:65) (1655)
Chingogan (Northumberland County Record Book 1652-1658:68) (1656)

CHINGOHAN

Creek: Northumberland County; originally applied to Presley Creek but later to Cod (Mottram) Creek; a tributary on the Potomac River's right side; defines the west side of Bay Quarter Neck.

Chingehan (PB 2:186) (1649)
Chickhan (PB 3:64) (1653)
Chuckahann (PB 3:64) (1653)
Chinkahan (PB 4:158) (1657)
Chinkakun (PB 4:563) (1657)
Chingoham (Northumberland County Record Book 1658-1662:19) (1658)
Chinghohan (PB 5:201) (1662)
Chinghohan (PB 5:201) (1662)
Chinkahun (PB 5:286) (1662)
Chinkahunn (PB 5:292) (1662)
Chingohan (PB 6:200) (1668)

CHIPEAKS

Creek: James City County; a tributary of Gordons or Checkerhouse Creek, which in turn is a tributary on the Chickahominy River's left side.

Chipeaks (PB 2:321) (1651)

CHIPPIAKE

Creek: Henrico County; a tributary on the James River's left side, east of the falls and approximately 2 miles west of Shockoe Creek.

Chippiake (PB 4:93) (1662)
Chippiack (William Byrd Title Book 103) (1663)

CHIPPOKES

Creek (Upper): part of the boundary between Surry and Prince George Counties; a tributary on the James River's right side.

Choopokes (PB 1:53) (1627)
Chippoackes (PB 1:124) (1633)
Chippoecks (PB 1:349) (1636)
Chippoeks (PB 1:546) (1638)
Chipoake (PB 2:35) (1645)
Chipoakes (PB 2:39) (1645)
Chipoaks (PB 2:111) (1647)
Chip Oakes (PB3:256) (1653)
Chepokes (PB 4:59) (1657)
Chapokes (PB 5:305) (1663)
Chipok (Herrman map) (1670)
Chippoax Creek (PB 9:439) (1702)
Chipoak (Fry-Jefferson map) (1751)
Chippoak (Donn map) (1873)

Creek (Lower): Surry County; a tributary on the James River's right side.

Chipoakes (PB 1:14) (1624)
Chippokes (PB 1:359) (1636)
Chipokes (PB 2:161) (1649)
Chipok (Herrman map) (1670)
Chipoak (Fry-Jefferson map) (1751)
Chippoak (Donn map) (1873)

Powhatan Indian Place Names in Tidewater Virginia

Indian Town: Surry County; inland from the right side of Upper Chippokes Creek.

Chawopo (Smith map) (1612)

Neck: Surry County; a neck of land between Upper Chippokes and Wards creeks.

Upper Chippoecks (PB 1:349) (1636)
Upper Chippokes (PB 1:490) (1637)

Place: Northumberland County; location uncertain.

Chippokoe (Northumberland County Wills, Inventories &c 1652-1658:127) (1657)

Places: Surry County; colloquial place name usually linked to the land near Upper or Lower Chippokes Creek; Upper Chippokes was upstream from Chippokes Point.

Chipoake (PB 2:4) (1643)
Chipoak (PB 2:81) (1646)
Chipoakes (PB 2:304) (1651)

Point: Surry County; a point just upstream from Upper Chippokes Creek.

Chippoak (Hilgarde map) (1882a)

CHISKIACK

Creek: York County; a tributary on the York River's right side; now called Indian Field Creek.

Kiskiack (Velasco map) (1610)
Chiskyake (PB 2:156) (1648)
Keeskiah (Langston map) (1662)

Creek: Gloucester County; a tributary on the Piankatank River's right side; now known as Ferry Creek.

Chiskyake (PB 2:165) (1648)
Chesecake (PB 5:192) (1662)
Cheeskake (Herrman map) (1670)
Chescake (PB 6:60) (1672)
Chiescake (PB 6:438) (1672)

Creek: Mathews County; a tributary on the Piankatank River's right side; now known as Wadinger Creek.

Tankes Cheskeyock (PB 1:798) (1642)

Indian Towns and Territory: York County; on the York River's right bank, downstream from Indian Field Creek; a king's house when the first colonists arrived; vacated by the Indians in 1622-1623 after retaliatory raids and displaced in 1629-1630. In ca. 1610, the chief's name was Ottahotin (HAILE 628).

Chescaik (BAR I:98) (1607)
Chesceyek (Tyndall map) (1608)
Kiskirk (CJS I:57) (1608)
Kiskieck (CJS I:63) (1608)
Kiskiack (Smith map) (1612)
Chiskact (CJS III:303) (1624)
Kiskyack (HEN I:141) (1629)
Chiscake (PB 1:369) (1630)
Chisekiake (PB 1:525) (1634)
Chiskeiake (PB 1:513) (1637)
Chiskiake (PB 1:513) (1637)
Chiskiacke (PB 1:513) (1637
Chiskiack (Vingboons map) (1639)
Chikiake (PB 1:740) (1642)
Chiskyake (PB 2:166) (1648)
Chickyack (PB 2:340) (1651)
Cheesecake (PB 3:31) (1652)
Cheesckiack (York County, Deeds, Wills

Powhatan Indian Place Names in Tidewater Virginia

and Orders 1: 139) (1652)
Chesceake (PB 6:72) 1667)

Indian Town: Gloucester and Mathews Counties; on the Piankatank River's right bank; area to which the Chiskiack Indians retreated after colonists took possession of their York River territory around 1629-1630. In 1649, their chief was Ossikacan (or Wassatickon); in 1655, the regent for his son and successor was named Pindavaco (or Pindeabank) (HAILE 628; PP 91, 117).

Chickyake (PB 2:340) (1651)
Chiscake (PB 3:122) (1652)
Cheescake (PB 3:122) (1652)
Chiskack (PB 3:203) (1652)
Chesskoiack (HEN II:39) (1661)
Chiskoiack (HEN II:39) (1661)
Chesquiack (HEN II:153) (1662)
Cheescake (Herrman map) (1670)
Chesscakedian (Herrman map) (1670)
Cheskyake (MCGC 401) (1675)
Kiskiack (Ogilby map) (1676)

Parish: York County; colonial parish established in 1640 and including the territory between Queens Creek and Morgan's Creek, a small, marshy inlet just west of Roosevelt (Brackens) Pond. In 1643 Chiskiack Parish was renamed Hampton Parish (DSVA 172-173).

Chiskiack (HEN I:223) (1640)
Chiskyak (PB 2:156) (1648)
Chesequack (York County, Deeds, Wills and Orders 1: 146) (1652)

Path: Gloucester and King and Queen Counties; located between the Poropotank and Mattaponi Rivers and extending northeastward to Ferry Creek on the Piankatank River.

Chiskayack (PB 3:94) (1652)
Cheeskake (PB 3:84) (1653)
Cheskyacke (PB 3:90) (1653)
Chiscake (PB 4:282) (1654)
Chescake (PB 4:314) (1661)
Chesecake (PB 5:192) (1662)
Cheskaak (PB 5:459) (1663)
Chescaack (PB 5:459) (1663)
Chiscaike (PB 6:172) (1665)
Chiscaiack (PB 6:301) (1670)
Chees Cake (PB 6:685) (1679)

CHOHUNCOCK

Branch: Prince George (formerly Charles City) County; a tributary on the Appomattox River's right side.

Chohuncock (PB 7:29) (1680)

CHOPAWAMSIC

Creek: part of the boundary between Stafford and Prince William Counties; a tributary on the Potomac River's right side.

Chapawansick (PB 3:228) (1653)
Chappawancy (PB 4:71) (1654)
Chappawansicke (PB 4:71) (1656)
Chapawansicke (PB 4:269) (1658)
Chappawansack (PB 5:208) (1664)
Chopawamsic (Fry-Jefferson map) (1751)
Chopowansic (Henry map) (1770)
Chopawamsic (Gilmer map) (186[-])
Styx (Young and Hesselbach map) (1862)

CHOSICKE

Indian Town: Charles City County; on the Chickahominy River's right bank, across from Chickahominy Haven;

Powhatan Indian Place Names in Tidewater Virginia

probably in the vicinity of Graves Landing.

Chosicke (Zuniga map) (1608)
Chosicks (Smith map) (1612)

CHOTANK

Creek: King George County; a tributary on the Potomac River's right side.

Chetanck (PB 2:246) (1650)
Chetank (PB 2:285) (1650)
Chotanke (Northumberland County Wills and Inventories 1652-1658:30) (1650)
Chotanks Northumberland County Wills and Inventories 1652-1658:30) (1650)
Chetanks (PB 4:237) (1658)
Chotanck (PB 4:177) (1658)
Chotank (PB 4:177) (1658)
Chotanks (PB 4:237) (1658)
Chotink (Fry-Jefferson map) (1751)
Chotank (Anonymous map) (1776)
Chotank (Tatham map) (1813)

Indian Town: King George County; on right bank of Chotank Creek, a tributary on the Potomac River's right side.

Chetanck (PB 2:285) (1650)
Chetank (PB 3:79) (1653)
Choetanck (PB 5:313) (1662)

CHOWOMAN

Branch: King George County; creek it flows into uncertain; ultimately a tributary on the Rappahannock River's left side, but two miles inland.

Chowman (Old Rappahannock County Deeds 1672-1676:59) (1672)
Chowoman (Old Rappahannock County Deeds and Wills 1677-1682:275) (1680)

CHUCKATUCK

Creek: City of Suffolk, formerly Nansemond County; a tributary on the James River's right side.

Chuck A Tuck (PB 1:505) (1637)
Chucka Tuck (PB 1:530) (1638)
Chucatuck (PB 1:611) (1638)
Chuckquotuck ([Old] Norfolk County, Minute Book 1637-1646:237) (1645)
Choketuck (PB 5:265) (1664)
Chuckatuck (PB 6:25) (1666)
Chuckey Tuck (PB 8:252) (1693)
Chuckeytuck (PB 8:255) (1693)
Chukkotuck (Herrman map) (1670)
Chuckatuck (Pierce map) (1872)

Place: modern village in City of Suffolk, formerly Nansemond County.

Chucatuck (Bache map) (1862c)

CINQUACK

Indian Town: Northumberland County; on the right bank of the Great Wicomico River's mouth, near Reedville; on the Chesapeake Bay.

Cinquaoteck (Zuniga map) (1608)
Cinquack (Smith map) (1612)
Cinoquak (Herrman map) (1670)

CINQUAETOCK

Indian Town: James City County; on the left bank of the Chickahominy River; near its mouth and just above Barrett's Point.

Cinquaetock (Zuniga map) (1608)

Powhatan Indian Place Names in Tidewater Virginia

CINQUOTECK

Indian Town: King William County; on the Pamunkey River's left bank, in the vicinity of Port Richmond, near West Point; a king's house.

Cinquaoteck (Zuniga map) (1608)
Cinquateck (Ogilby map) (1676)

COHOKE

Creek, Swamp, and Marsh: King William County; a tributary on the Pamunkey River's left side.

Cohoake (PB 3:34) (1653)
Chohoake (PB 3:59) (1653)
Cohoke (PB 4:145) (1657)
Cohookoke (PB 6:294) (1670)
Cohoak (Herrman map) (1676)
Nicatawance (PB 9:260) (1700)
Niccatiwanse (PB 10:49) (1711)

COMISTANCK

Branch: King George County; a tributary on the Rappahannock River's left side, near a swamp and Weequionedike Branch; probably near the Nanzattico Indians' town.

Comistanck (PB 5:536) (1665)

COMPEKEEKE

Creek: Northampton County; a tributary of Occohannock Creek; possibly present Killman Cove.

Compekeeke (PB 2:159) (1648)

CONECOCKS

Brook: Chesterfield (formerly Henrico) County; a tributary on the Appomattox River's left side, near Powells (now Shands) Creek.

Conecocks (PB 3:32) (1652)
Cotnecocks (PB 3:32) (1652)
Conecock (PB 3:41) (1652)

Path: Chesterfield (formerly Henrico) County; near Cole's Swamp.

Cunicott (PB 2:262) (1650)

Swamp: Chesterfield (formerly Henrico) County; a low-lying area west of Point of Rocks.

Kennecock (PB 1:839) (1642)

CONJURER'S FIELD

Marsh: Chesterfield County; low-lying area along the Appomattox River's left side; upstream from Swift Creek.

Conjurer's Field (PB 1:300) (1635)

CONJURING POINT

Point: Charles City County; on the James River's left bank near its junction with the Chickahominy River; just south of Tomahund Creek's mouth; later known as Juring Point and now known as During Point.

Conjuring Point (PB 1:137) (1632)

COPAMCO

Bay and Island: Accomack County;

near Chesconnessex Creek and the Chesapeake Bay.

Copamco (PB 9:716) (1702)

COPPAHAUNK

Branch and Swamp: Sussex County; a tributary on the Blackwater River's right side; midway between Waverly and Windsor, with the headwaters are near modern Dendron.

Coppahaunk (PB 9:325) (1701)
Coskoraw (PB 9:332) (1701)
Coppohonk (PB 9:336) (1701)
Coshunkoraw (PB 10:153) (1714)
Cappahonk (PB 10:264) (1715)
Coppohunk (Boye map) (1826)
Toppahank (Bache map) (1862c)

Indian Town: Surry or Sussex County; near the Blackwater River in its upper reaches; a village occupied by either the Weyanock or the Pochick-Nansemond Indians in 1664.

Coppahunck (Surry County, Orders 1671-1691: 2) (1672)
Coppahaunk (Stanard, "Indians of Southern Virginia" [conclusion], 4) (1710)

CORONEESAW

Swamp: Sussex (formerly Surry) County; a tributary on the Nottoway River's right side.

Coroneesaw Swamp (PB 13:366) (1727)

CORRATTAWOMEN

Branch and Creek: Accomack County; a tributary of the Atlantic Ocean; said to be near Occoconson, a place at the head of Occohannock Creek.

Corrattawomen (PB 4:122) (1664)
Corrattawaman (PB 5:187) (1664)
Curratowoman (PB 5:489) (1666)

CORROTOMAN

Bay: Lancaster County; at the mouth of the Corrotoman River, on the Rappahannock River's left side.

Cortoman (PB 2:253 (1650)

Creek: boundary line between Lancaster and Northumberland Counties; a tributary of Fleets Bay; interchangeably known as Chesticon or Corrotoman Creek; by the mid-eighteenth century, known as Indian Creek.

Corrotomen (PB 4:81) (1656)
Corotomon (PB 4:130) (1657)
Corrotoman (PB 4:238) (1658)
Chesticond (PB 4:382) (1658)
Chesticon (PB 4:311) (1662)
Coratoman (PB 4:311) (1662)
Currotomon (Jefferson-Brooke map) (1747)

Creek: Lancaster County; a tributary on the Rappahannock River's left side; now known as Carters Creek.

Cossatomen (PB 1:804) (1642)
Cassatawoman (PB 1:882) 1643)
Cosotawaman (PB 3:188) (1652)

Indian Town: King George County; on the Rappahannock River's left bank, in the vicinity of Hop Yard Landing, above Popcastle Turn; a king's house.

Cuttatawomen (Velasco map) (1610)

Powhatan Indian Place Names in Tidewater Virginia

Cuttatawoman (Smith map) (1612)

Indian Town: Lancaster County; on the Rappahannock River's left bank, downstream from Mosquito Point; a king's house.

Cuttatawomen (CJS I:53) (1608)
Cuttatawoman (Smith map) (1612)

Indian Town: Northumberland County; on the left bank of Indian Creek, a tributary of Fleets Bay; occupied from 1656 through at least the 1670s.

Corotomen (PB 4:82) 1656)

Indian Town: Northumberland County; on the Great Wicomico River's right side, near the Chesapeake Bay; possibly on Harvey's Neck.

Cattalowman (PB 2:183) (1649)

Place: Northumberland County; location mentioned in a patent for land on the lower branches of the Great Wicomico River; probably on the west side of Barrett Creek.

Corrotoman (PB 4:240) (1658)

Point: Lancaster County; east of the Corrotoman River's mouth, on the Rappahannock River's left side, near Weems.

Curratoman (Bache map) (1857c)

River: Lancaster County; a tributary on the Rappahannock River's left side; flanked by Weems and Towles Point.

Curritomon (PB 2:202) (1649)
Corotomen (PB 2:253) (1650)
Coritomen (PB 2:259) (1650)
Curytomon (PB 2:308) (1650)
Corytomon (PB 2:308) (1650)
Corotomon (PB 2:335) (1651)
Cattatawoman (PB 3:163) (1652)
Cattowoman (PB 3:167) (1652)
Corocoman (PB 3:343) (1655)
Coratowamon (PB 4:5) (1655)
Cuttatoman (Northumberland County Wills and Inventories 1652-1658:61) (1655)
Corrotoman (PB 4:59) (1656)
Cottawoman (PB 5:339) (1662)
Coratoman (PB 5:141) (1664)
Corattoman (PB 5:405) (1665)
Coretoman (PB 6:260) (1669)
Currotoman (PB 6:635) (1678)
Curratoman (Fry-Jefferson map) (1751)

COSS COSS

Creek: Westmoreland County; a tributary of the Nomini River; probably present Pierce Creek.

Cos Cosh (Westmoreland County, Deeds and Wills 1:168) (1662)
Cose Coss (PB 5:395) (1664)
Coss Coss (PB 5:159) (1665)

COTCHAWESCO

Place: unidentifiable county; at the head of a tributary of Meherrin River; occupied by the Weyanock Indians in 1675.

Catchawesco (Stanard, "Indians of Southern Virginia," 350) (1710)
Cotchawesco (Stanard, "Indians of Southern Virginia," [conclusion], 5) (1710)
Cotchawesk (Stanard, "Indians of Southern Virginia," [conclusion], 6) (1710)

Powhatan Indian Place Names in Tidewater Virginia

COTCSHUROH

Branch: Prince George (formerly Charles City) County; a tributary on the Nottoway River's left side; near Jones Hole Swamp.

Cotcshuroh (PB 9:337) (1701)
Ante Shuroh (PB 9:337) (1701)

COTTESHORAW

Branch: Surry County; a tributary on the left side of Blackwater Swamp; near the line between Prince George and Surry counties.

Cotteshoraw (PB 10:311) (1711)

COUSIAC

Creek and Marsh: New Kent County; a tributary on the Pamunkey River's right side; present Mill Creek and Cooks Mill Pond.

Tanks Queens (Langston map) (1662)
Cawjick (Herrman map) (1670)

COWAWOMAN

Path: Northumberland County; a trail on the lower side of the Potomac River; near Hollowes Creek.

Cowawoman (Northumberland County Wills and Inventories 1652-1658:3) (1651)

CURRAWAUGH

Place: City of Suffolk (formerly Nansemond County); location also known as New Dursley; on the west side of Dismal Swamp and near the headwaters of the Nansemond River; site of English fortifications built in March 1676 on the eve of Bacon's Rebellion.

Currawaugh (HEN II:328-329) (1676)

Swamp: Isle of Wight County; a tributary of the Blackwater River.

Currowah (PB 9:166) (1698)
Corowaugh (PB 10:41) (1711)
Corrowaugh (Boye map) (1826)

CURRIOMAN

Bay: Westmoreland County; on the right side of the Potomac River; west of Nomini Bay; near Currioman Landing.

Conwoman (PB 2:337) (1651)
Connawoman (PB 3:67) (1653)
Conawoman (PB 7:459) (1662)

Cliffs: Westmoreland County; on the right side Potomac River; at the head of Cat Point (formerly Great Rappahannock) Creek; probably present Horsehead Cliffs.

Corowoman (PB 3:357) (1655)
Curawoman (PB 5:364) (1664)

Creek: Westmoreland County; a tributary on the Potomac River's right side; flows into Currioman Bay; near Brent Town.

Conawoman (PB 2:249) (1650)
Canawoman (PB 2:282) (1650)
Connawoman (PB 3:67) (1653)
Corewoman (PB 5:389) (1664)
Corawoman (PB 6:107) (1672)

Powhatan Indian Place Names in Tidewater Virginia

CURRITUCK

Creek: Accomack County; stream now known as Craddock Creek; a tributary of the Chesapeake Bay, just south of present Nandua Creek.

Craducks (PB 2:365) (1644)
Currituck (PB 2:178) (1649)
Craddockes (PB 2:178) (1649)
Cradicks (PB2:179) (1649)
Corratock (PB 2:326) (1651)
Coratock (PB 3:111) (1652)
Curratuck (PB 3:257) (1652)
Curratocke (PB 4:53) (1658)
Caratocke (PB 4:139) (1658)
Corrattuck (Accomack County, Deeds and Wills 1664-1671:43) (1666)
Corotoke (PB 6:306) (1670)
Choratucke (Accomack County Deeds Orders and Wills 1673-1675:141) (1674)
Corrotuck (PB 7:641) (1688)
Curretick (PB 7:641) (1688)
Cradick (Fry-Jefferson map) (1751)
Cradick (Henry map) (1770)

CUSTIPA

Place: New Kent County; somewhere in the headwaters of Chickahominy River.

Custipa (PB 1:640) (1639)

DANCING POINT

Point: Charles City County; on the James River's left bank, just west of the junction of the James and Chickahominy Rivers; near one of two Chickahominy Indian towns called Paspahegh.
Dancing Point (PB 1:53) (1627)

DIASCUND

Creek: part of the boundary between James City and New Kent Counties; a tributary on the Chickahominy River's left side; the creek's headwaters became known as Wahrani.

Tyascan (PB 3:37) (1653)
Tyascun (PB 4:7) (1655)
Tyoscun (PB 4:261 (1658)
Tyascum (PB 5:374) (1664)
Tyascunn (PB 7:445) (1685)
Dias Kons (Captaine map) (1781)
Diascun (Jefferson map) (1787)

Place: James City County; on the Chickahominy River's left bank, east of Diascund Creek; possibly the former site of the Indian town called Ozenick, located near Uncles Neck and Hog Neck.

Tyascun (PB 3:266) (1654)
Tyascum (PB 3:381) (1656)
Tyascon (PB 4:284) (1661)

Swamp: New Kent County; the headwaters of the creek of the same name.

Diascun (PB 4:76) (1656)
Tyascun (PB 4:80) (1656)
Dieiscum (PB 4:151) (1658)
Tyascond (PB 4:219) (1658)
Diascunn (PB 4:255) (1658)
Tyoscun (PB 4:261) (1658)
Tyascunn (PB 4:261) (1658)
Dyascun (PB 4:326) (1662)
Tyascum (PB 5:365) (1662)
Tyescun (PB 7:22) (1680)
Tiascunn (PB 8:322) (1694)

DOGUE

Branch: King William (later Caroline) County; located above the splitting of the

Powhatan Indian Place Names in Tidewater Virginia

Mattaponi River; near the old Doeg Indian town.

Doeg (PB 10:372) (1718)

Creek: Fairfax County; a tributary on the Potomac River's right side, near Mount Vernon.

Doegs (PB 4:112) (1664)
Epsewassen (Stafford County Record Book 1686-1693:196) (1690)
Dogney (Fry-Jefferson map) (1751)

Indian Town: Maryland; on the Potomac River's left bank; opposite Sandy or Ragged (Raggett) Point in Westmoreland County; used as a reference point in Virginia patents.

Dauges (PB 4:70) (1654)
Doges (PB 3:284) (1654)
Doegs (PB 3:170) (1657)

Indian Town: King George (formerly Stafford) County; on the Rappahannock River's left bank between Millbank Creek and Dogue Run; near the sites of the towns known as Monanask and Waconask.

Doegs (PB 5:160) (1664)
Doagge (Old Rappahannock County, Deeds 3:58) (1666)
Doeggs (PB 5:509) (1666)
Doogs (Herrman map) (1670)
Tacci alias Dogi (LED 10) (1672)

Indian Town: Prince William County; on the Potomac River's right bank, at the junction with Occoquan Bay; the village was known as May-umps; located on Dogue Island.

May-umps (VCR III:73) (1617)

Indian Town: probably Stafford County; somewhere along the Potomac River's left bank.

Doegs (Stafford County Records 1664-1668, 1689-1693:200) (1691)

Indian Town: King William (later Caroline) County; located near the splitting of the Mattaponi River into the Matta, Po, and Ni Rivers.

Doeg (PB 10:162) (1714)
Doeg (PB 10:372) (1718)

Island: Prince William County; a now-submerged island at the junction of the Potomac River and Occoquan Bay; known as Miompses Island during the 1650s and 1660s.

Miompses (PB 3:68) (1653)
Doages (PB 4:92) (1657)
Myampses (PB 4:450) (1660)
Dogs (PB 4:450) (1660)
Doegs (PB 3:297) (1662)
Doege (PB 5:422) (1665)
Doegs (Stafford County, Will Book Z:250) (1701)
Doggs (PB 2:333) (1651)

Path: King George County; a trail that ran between the Rappahannock River's left bank and the Potomac River's right bank, passing near the headwaters of Passapatanzy Creek.

Doeggs (PB 5:271) (1663)
Doegs (PB 6:122) (1668)

Run: King George County; a tributary on the Rappahannock River's left side; near Keys Run Creek and the modern community known as Dogue.

Powhatan Indian Place Names in Tidewater Virginia

Dogue (USGS Fredericksburg quadrangle) (1888)

EACKATONKE

Place: City of Suffolk, formerly Nansemond County; near the western branch of the Nansemond River; location uncertain.

Eackatonke (PB 5:300) (1663)

EKEKS

Branch: Accomack County; a tributary of Onancock Creek's southerly branch.

Ekeks (PB 4:1) (1655)
Ekeeks (PB 4:461) (1660)
Ekouks (Accomack County, Wills 1673-1676: 344) (1675)

ENOCOMOE

Place: Northumberland County; probably near Cherry Point Neck.

Enocomoe (Northumberland County Order Book 1652-1665:14) (1652)

GENITO

Creek: Goochland (formerly Henrico) County; a tributary on the James River's left side near Crozier. (May not be an Algonquian name.)

Gennitoe (PB 9:525) (1703)
Genito PB 10:161) (1714)
Jenitoe (PB 10:216) (1714)
Giney-Towe (PB 10:237) (1715)
Jenny-Toe (PB 10:420) (1719)
Jennyroe (PB 10:423) (1719)
Jennestoe (PB 11:240) (1723)
Jinnetoe (PB 12:126) (1724)
Jenetoe (PB 12:230) (1725)
Jennito (PB 14:334) (1734)
Geneto (PB 14:334) (1734)
Jenetoe (Fry-Jefferson map) (1751)
Genito (LaPrade map) (1880)

Creek: Brunswick County; a tributary on the Meherrin River's right bank, near Watkins Corner. (May not be an Algonquian name.)

Geneto (PB 14:88) (1728)
Jeneto (PB 14:305) (1731)

GIBSEY

Creek: Richmond County; toward the head of Cat Point (formerly Great Rappahannock or Rappahannock) Creek, itself a tributary on the Rappahannock River's left side; land patents state that the Indians called the creek Gibsey or Gibson.

Gibson (PB 4:123) (1655)
Gibsey (PB 4:464) (1661)

GINGASKIN

Indian Town: Northampton County; east of Eastville, on the Indian Town Creek's right bank; in December 1640 a 1,500 acre patent was given to the Accomac Indians as a preserve or reservation. After the Accomacs moved there, they became known as the Gingaskins.

Powhatan Indian Place Names in Tidewater Virginia

Gingaskoyne (Northampton County, Deeds, Wills and Orders 3: 219) (1650)
Chingaskin (Northampton County, Orders 9:48) (1668)
Chingoskin (MCGC 353) (1673)
Gingas King (PB 7:49) (1680)
Gingase (Bruce, "Public Officers in Virginia," 363)
Gangascoe (BEV 232) (1705)
Gingas King (Northampton County, Orders 15: 86) (1712)
Gingasking (Northampton County, Orders 30: 246) (1785)
Gingaskin (PB 7:49) (1680)
Indian Town (Northampton County Plat Book, survey #37) (1813)

GINGOTEAGUE

Branch and Creek: King George and Richmond Counties; a tributary on the Rappahannock River's left side, east of Port Conway.

Gingoatege (PB 6:120) (1668)
Ginquatuck (Herrman map) (1670)
Gingoetege (PB 6:514) (1674)
Chingatague (PB 7:34) (1680)
Gingoteak (Old Rappahannock County Deeds and Wills 1677-1682:263) (1679)
Quingatengue (Richmond County Deed Book 1 [1692-1693]:117-118) (1689)
Chingateague (Richmond County Deed Book 2 [1693-1695]:200 (1696)
Chingoteague (Jefferson-Brooke map) (1747)

Swamp: the headwaters of Gingoteague Creek.

Jengateague (Richmond County Deed Book 2 [1693-1695]:142-144) (1695)

HEARTQUAKE

Creek: King and Queen County; on the Mattaponi River's left side, west of Little Plymouth.

Hartquake (PB 7:213) (1682)
Heartquakue (PB 7:213) (1682)
Hartquip (Captaine map) (1781)

Swamp: King and Queen County; on the Mattaponi River's left side; the headwaters of Heartquake Creek.

Hartequack (PB 5:253) (1665)
Hartquack (PB 5:418) (1665)
Harkquack (PB 5:458) (1665)
Hartquake (PB 6:513) (1674)
Hathquake (PB 7:33) (1680)
Hartquin (Fry-Jefferson map) (1751)

HUNGARS

Creek: Northampton County; a tributary of the Chesapeake Bay.

Hungers (PB 1:182) (1635)
Hungar (PB 1:286) (1635)
Hungars (PB 1:434) (1637)
Hongers (PB 6:253) (1669)
Hunger (Fry-Jefferson map) (1751)
Hengers (Anonymous map) (1776)

HUNKEPEN

Point: New Kent County; on the Pamunkey River's right bank, near present Cattail Swamp and Black Creek.

Hauke Pen (PB 3:243) (1653)
Hunkepen (PB 5:279) (1653)

Powhatan Indian Place Names in Tidewater Virginia

HUSQUAMPS

Place: Isle of Wight County; land "known by an Indian name of Husquamps;" located approximately four miles up the Pagan River, near Smithfield.

Husquamps (PB 1:407) (1636)

INDIAN BRIDGE

Place: Accomack County; Indian-built footbridge over Pungoteague Creek or one of its tributaries.

Indian Bridge (PB 3:12) (1654)

Place: Lancaster County; Indian-built footbridge over a swamp in the headwaters of the Corrotoman River.

Indian Bridge (PB 5:249) (1664)

Place: Northampton County; Indian-built footbridge at head of Occohannock Creek.

Indian Bridge (PB 2:272) (1650)

Place: City of Virginia Beach (formerly Princess Anne County); Indian-built footbridge in the vicinity of the Lynnhaven River.

Indian Bridge (PB 2:126) (1648)

Place: York County; Indian-built footbridge near the Chiskiack Indians' old town; probably near Indian Field Creek.

Indian Bridge (PB 2:316) (1651)

INDIAN BRANCH

Branch: Gloucester County; a swamp at the head of the Ware River; probably Beaverdam Swamp.

Indian Branch (PB 5:291) (1663)

INDIAN BURYING GROUND

Place: Dinwiddie County; the Appomattox River's right bank; near Broad Falls.

Burying Ground (Boye map) (1826)

INDIAN CABIN

Branch: City of Virginia Beach (formerly Princess Anne County); a branch of Long Creek, a tributary of the right side of the Lynnhaven River.

Indian Cabin (Lower Norfolk County, Wills and Deeds 1646-1651:49) (1647)
Indian Cabin (PB 5:411) (1665)

Neck: York and James City Counties; between the headwaters of Queens Creek and Long Hill Swamp.

Indian Neck (PB 5:390) (1653)

Neck: City of Virginia Beach (formerly Princess Anne County); near the head of the Lynnhaven River.

Indian Neck (Lower Norfolk County, Wills and Deeds 1666-1675: 145) (1673)

INDIAN CREEK

Creek: Louisa (formerly Hanover)

Powhatan Indian Place Names in Tidewater Virginia

County; a tributary on the South Anna River's left side; west of Cattail Creek; near Cuckoo and Apple Grove. These Indians were not the Algonquian-speaking Powhatans.

Indian Creek (Captaine map) (1781)

Creek: Richmond County; on the Rappahannock River's left side; possibly an earlier name for Rappahannock (now Cat Point) Creek.

Indian Creek (PB 2:213) (1650)

Creek: City of Chesapeake (formerly Norfolk County); a tributary on the left side of the Eastern Branch of the Elizabeth River; probably same as modern Indian River.

Indian Creek (PB 1:603) (1638)

Creek: Northumberland County; a tributary of Fleets Bay.

Indian Creek (Fry-Jefferson map) (1751)

Creek: City of Suffolk (formerly Nansemond County); a tributary at the head of the Nansemond River's Western Branch; probably now in the vicinity of Lake Prince.

Indian Creek (PB 1:765) (1640)

Creek: City of Virginia Beach (formerly Princess Anne County); a tributary on the Lynnhaven River's left side.

Indian Creek (PB 1:327) (1635)

INDIAN FIELD

Creek: York County; a tributary on the York River's right side; originally known as Chiskiack or Keeskiah Creek and Digges Creek; now known as Indian Field Creek.

Indian Field (Bache map, 1857b)

Neck: Isle of Wight County; east of a brook known as the Indian Snares; probably downstream from the town of Smithfield.

Indian Neck (PB 1:502) (1637)

Neck: Lancaster County; present Fleets Bay Neck; between Indian and Dymer Creeks.

Indian Neck (PB 2:206) (1649)

Path: New Kent County; on the York River's right bank; a trail between Ware Creek and Wahrani Swamp, near the head of Diascund Creek.

Indian Path (PB 5:359) (1663)

INDIAN FERRY

Ferry: King William and King and Queen Counties; a crossing between Chelsea Farm, in King William, and the mouth of Old Mill Creek.

Indian Ferry (PB 3:4) (1653)

INDIAN FORT

Place: King William County; on the Pamunkey River's left bank; upstream from Manquin Creek; also known as the Manskin fort (q.v.) and as Fort Royall,

Powhatan Indian Place Names in Tidewater Virginia

established by the Virginia government in 1645.

Indian Fort (Langston map) (1662)
Manaskin Fort (PB 5:370) (1664)

INDIAN HOUSE THICKET

Place: City of Hampton (formerly Elizabeth City County); a neck of land, the site of a European settlement, on the Hampton River's left bank during the early-to-mid 1620s. Possibly in the vicinity of Hampton University.

Indian House Thicket (PB 1:77) (1626)

INDIAN PATH

Path: City of Virginia Beach; a trail running across a tributary of the Lynnhaven River;

Indian Path (Lower Norfolk County, Wills and Deeds 1651-1656:15) (1652)

Road: Gloucester County; a trail in the northeastern part the county, in Ware Parish, and extending toward the North River.

Indian Road (PB 6:130) (1668)

INDIAN POINT

Point: Northumberland County; on the Great Wicomico River's right bank, upstream from Knight Run.

Indian Point (USGS Heathville quadrangle) (1917)

Point: Prince George County; on the James River's right bank, east of Tar Bay at Coggins Point.

Indian Point (Gilmer map) (1864c).

Point: City of Suffolk; probably adjacent to Western Branch of the Nansemond River (formerly known as the Indian Branch) and Lake Prince.

Indian Point (PB 3:215) (1653)

INDIAN QUARTER

Creek: Gloucester County; a tributary on the York River's left side; somewhere in the eastern part of the county.

Indian Quarter (PB 1:800) (1642)

INDIAN RIVER

River: City of Chesapeake (formerly Norfolk County); a tributary on the left side of the Eastern Branch of the Elizabeth River; probably the same as Indian Creek.

INDIAN SNARES

Brook: Isle of Wight County; probably modern Brewer's Creek, a tributary on Chickatuck Creek's left side.

Indian Snares (PB 1:502) (1637)

INDIAN SPRING

Spring: Gloucester County; near the head of the Poropotank River.

Indian Spring (PB 1:502) (1642)

Spring: City of Hampton (formerly Elizabeth City County); near the location that in 1633 was known as "ffox hill" and Point Comfort (now Mill) Creek.

Powhatan Indian Place Names in Tidewater Virginia

Indian Spring (PB 1:123) (1633)

Spring: Isle of Wight County; on the James River's right bank; near the Pagan River.

Indian Spring (PB 4:25) (1655)

Spring: Lancaster County; somewhere on the Corrotoman River.

Indian Spring (PB 2:308) (1650)

Spring: York County; on the York River's right bank; northeast of Middle Plantation, later known as Williamsburg.

Indian Spring (PB 2:94) (1646)

Swamp: Sussex (formerly Surry) County; probably a tributary of the Blackwater River.

Indian Spring (PB 5:194) (1664)

INDIAN STONE

Place: City of Hampton (formerly Elizabeth City County); stone (no description recorded) found near Old Point Comfort Island (now Fort Monroe).

Indian Stone (PB 1:334) (1635)

INDIAN SWAMP

Swamp: James City County; somewhere in the Chickahominy River's lower reaches.

Indian Swamp (PB 4:7) (1655)

INDIAN TOWN

Branch: City of Norfolk (formerly Norfolk County); a tributary at the head of the Lafayette River, formerly known as Daniel Tanners (or Tanner's) Creek.

Indian Town (PB 3:241) (1653)

Community: King William County; same as the Pamunkey Indian Reservation on the Pamunkey River's left bank. The name remained in use colloquially up through the 19th century.

Indian Town (Henry map) (1770)

Community: King William County; same as the Mattaponi Indian Reservation on the Mattaponi River's right bank. The name remained in use colloquially up through the 19th century.

Indian Town (Gilmer map) (1864b).

Creek: Dinwiddie County; on the Appomattox River's right bank; the boundary line between Petersburg and Dinwiddie County.

Indian Town (Boye map) (1826)
Old Town (USGS Petersburg quadrangle) (1892)

Creek: Northampton County; a tributary of Ramshorn Channel, located to the east of Eastville; formed the northern boundary of the Gingaskin Indian Reservation, which survived until 1813.

Indian Town (Northampton County Plat Book, survey #37) (1813)

Powhatan Indian Place Names in Tidewater Virginia

Island: Essex County; east side of Portobago Bay and west side of Green Bay.

Indian Town (Essex County Deeds and Wills 1711-1714:1) (1704)

Neck: Northampton County; neck on the Indian Town Creek's right bank; site of the old Gingaskin Indian Reservation.

Indian Town Neck (Northampton County Plat Book, survey #37) (1813)

Point: City of Norfolk (formerly Norfolk County); located on Indian Town Branch (q.v.).

Indian Town (PB 4:19) (1656)

Swamp: King William County; a tributary on the Mattaponi River's right side; forms the western boundary of the Mattaponi Indian Reservation, adjoining Shanty Creek.

Indian Town (USGS King and Queen quadrangle) (1985)

INDIAN WEIR

Place: King and Queen County; on the Mattaponi River's left bank, probably near Jones Landing.

Indian Weir (PB 6:502) (1674)

JOHNCHECOHUNK

Swamp: Surry County; a tributary on the right side of Cypress Swamp, itself a tributary on the Blackwater River's left side.

John Chokuck (PB 7:367) (1684)
John Checokuck (PB 7:369) (1684)
Johnchecohunk (PB 7:376) (1684)
Johnchohocunk (PB 7:376) (1684)
John Chehockan (PB 7:463) (1685)
Johnchounk (PB 7:691) (1688)
John Chehocon (PB 8:4) (1689)

KAPAWNICH

Indian Town: Lancaster County; on the Rappahannock River's left bank, probably west of the State Route 3 (Robert C. Norris) bridge, between Carters Creek and Corrotoman River.

Kapawnich (Smith map) (1612)

KAPOSEPOCK

Indian Town: King William or New Kent County; somewhere along the Pamunkey River. In ca. 1610, Weyamat was the chief in this town (HAILE 628).

Kaposepock (HAILE 628) (1612)

KECOUGHTAN

Indian Town: City of Hampton (formerly Elizabeth City County); on the left side of the Hampton River's mouth; on the grounds of the Veterans Administration Hospital. In 1607, the tribe's chief was Pochins, a son of Powhatan (HAILE 626).

Kegquohtan (CJS I:35) (1608)

Powhatan Indian Place Names in Tidewater Virginia

Kequoughtan (CJS I:53) (1608)
Kekowhatan (HAILE 512) (1610)
Kecotan (Velasco map) (1610)
Kecoughtan (Smith map) (1612)
Kekowhaton (HAILE 503) (1612)
Kiccowtan (VCR III:100) (1618)
Kiccoughtan (PB 1:2) ([1620-1624])
Kickoghtan (VCR III:612) (1622)
Kecougtan (CJS III:169) (1624)
Kekoughtan (CJS III:264) (1624)
Kecoughton (CJS III:323) (1624)
Kiquotan (PB 1:477) (1626)
Kickotan (PB 1:148) (1633)
Kecoghtan (Vingboons map) (1639)
Kequotan (PB 2:142) (1648)

Parish: City of Hampton (formerly Elizabeth City County); formed in 1610; extinct in 1619 when Elizabeth City Parish was formed (DSVA 110-113, 195).

Kiccowtan (JHB 1619-1660:7) (1619)

Place: City of Hampton (formerly Elizabeth City County, established in 1634); originally known as Kecoughtan, one of Virginia's four corporations, created by law in 1619.

Kecoughtan (JHB 1619-1660:7) (1619)
Kiccoughtan (PB 1:26) (1624)

Place: Northumberland County; somewhere on the Potomac River's right bank.

Kecotan (Northumberland County Wills, Inventories &c. 1652-1658:66) (1655)

River: City of Hampton (formerly Elizabeth City County); now called the Back River.

Kequotan (Lower Norfolk County Minute Book 1637-1646:4) (1637)

KEGOTANK

Bay: Accomack County; a bay located between Assawoman Island and the mainland; on the seaboard.

Kegotank (USCS Wallops and Assawoman Islands map) (1851)

Creek: Accomack County; a tributary of Kegotank Bay and Northam Narrows, behind Assawoman Island; on the seaboard.

Kisquotan (PB 4:92) (1663)
Kisquotancke (PB 4:92) (1663)
Kickcotanck (PB 5:184) (1664)
Kecqotank (PB 6:80) (1667)
Kikotan (Herrman map) (1670)
Kicotanke (PB 6:392) (1671)
Qiquotanck (Accomack County, Wills 1673-1676: 285) (1675)
Kickatanck (Accomack County, Wills 1673-1676: 314) (1675)
Kikotan (Fry-Jefferson map) (1751)

Indian Town: Accomack County; probably near Kegotank Creek and Kegotank Bay.

Kickotank (FOR III:10:30) (1649)
Kikotanke (Northampton County, Deeds, Wills and Orders 3: 217) (1650)
Kecotanke (PB 5:273) (1663)
Keokotanck (PB 6:483) (1673)
Kiquotank (Bruce, "Public Officers in Virginia, 1702, 1714," 363) (1702)
Kiequotank (BEV 232) (1704)

Place: Accomack County; vicinity of Kegotank Creek and Muddy Creek's head, near the seaboard.

Powhatan Indian Place Names in Tidewater Virginia

Kecotanke (PB 5:273) (1663)

KERAHOCAK

Indian Town: Westmoreland County; on the Rappahannock River's left bank; near Blind Point and Jetts Creek's mouth; opposite Baylor's Creek.

Kerahocak (Smith map) (1612)

KESEOKENSEEKE

Swamp: New Kent (formerly James City) County; on the Chickahominy River's left side; in the vicinity of Crump Swamp.

Keseokenseeke (PB 4:52) (1656)

KIMAGES

Creek: Charles City County; a tributary on the James River's left side near Camp Weyanoke; the lower part of creek has been dammed to create Charles Lake.

Kimiges (PB 1:282) (1635)
Kimodges (William Byrd Title Book 274) (ca. 1675)

KINGCOPSICO

Point: Westmoreland County; on the Potomac River's right bank, in Machodoc Neck, on the east side of Nomini Bay.

Kingcopsco (Jefferson-Brooke map) (1747)

KITTAWAN

Branch or Creek: Charles City County; on the left side of the James River; between Weyanoke Point and Mapsico Creek.

Kittawan (PB 5:436) (1665)
Kittewan Creek (PB 10:46) (1711)

KUPKIPCOCK

Indian Town: King William County; king's house; on the Pamunkey River's left bank, east of Sweet Hall Landing; immediately upstream was a small Indian town for which Captain John Smith failed to supply a name.

Kupkipcock (Smith map) (1612)

LAICHECOHANCK

Neck: Northumberland County; a neck of land between the branches of an unnamed creek southwest of Newman's Neck.

Laichecohanck (Northumberland County Wills, Inventories &c. 1652-1658:62). (1655)

MACCOSONECK

Creek: Sussex and Dinwiddie Counties (formerly Prince George); a tributary on the Nottoway River's left side; near Jones Hole and Rowanty Swamps.

Moccosoneck Creek (PB 9:714) (1706)
Maccosoneck Creek (PB 10:403) (1718)

Powhatan Indian Place Names in Tidewater Virginia

MACHACOMICO

Swamp: King William County; a tributary on the Mattaponi River's right side in the vicinity of Herring Creek.

Machacomico (PB 9:559) (1703)

MACHEZAN

Place: Westmoreland County; caves on the upperpart of Chopawamsick Creek.

Machezan (PB 4:321) (1662)

MACHIMEDES

Creek and Swamp: part of the boundary between James City and New Kent Counties; a tributary on the York River's right side; now known as Ware Creek.

Matchemeed (PB 3:5) (1653)
Matchemeeds (PB 3:323) (1654)
Matchemeedes (Langston map) (1662)
Mathemeed (PB 5:314) (1663)
Mashemeads (PB 7:312) (1683)

Place: eastern New Kent County; on the York River's right bank; land between Mill (Tankes Queens) and Ware (Matchemeedes) Creeks.

Machimedes (Langston map) (1662)
Mathomeedes (Bassett Family Papers, deed, Robert Abrahall to William Bassett) (1668)

MACHIPONGO

Branch: Northampton County; likely the upper reaches of the Machipongo River.

Machepungo Beaver Dam (PB 5:490) (1666)
Matchapungo Beaver Dam (PB 6:431) (1672)

Creek: King and Queen (formerly Gloucester) County; a tributary on the Mattaponi River's left side; probably Garretts Creek.

Matchepongo (PB 3:213) (1653)
Mathapungo (PB 7:32) (1680)

Creek: Middlesex (formerly Lancaster) County; a tributary on the Rappahannock River's right side; near the Piankatank River's upper reaches; probably near Urbanna.

Matchepungo (PB 3:15) (1653)

Creek: part of the boundary between Northampton and Accomack Counties; sometimes known as Parting Creek; a tributary of the Machipongo River, which flows into the Atlantic Ocean.

Matchepungo (PB 2:134) (1647)
Machepungo (Northampton County Deeds, Wills, Etc. 1708-1717:1) (1708)
Matchopungo (Northampton County Wills and Inventories, 1740-1750:336) (1748)

Indian Town: Accomack County; near the Machipongo River; possibly in the vicinity of Upshur Neck, or near Willis Wharf.

Matchepongo (PB 3:138) (1652)
Mathepongoe (PB 3:246) (1653)
Matchepungoe (PB 4:30) (1655)
Matchepungo (PB 4:466) (1661)
Machepungo (PB 5:373) (1664)
Mathapungo (PB 6:430) (1672)

Powhatan Indian Place Names in Tidewater Virginia

Machapungo (Bruce, "Public Officers in Virginia, 1702, 1714," 363) (1702)

Indian Town: Stafford County; on the Potomac River's right bank; possibly the same village as Mattacunt, identified by Captain John Smith in 1610.

Matchipongo (HAILE 658) (1612)

Island: Northampton County; at the dividing line between Accomack and Northampton Counties; possibly modern Bell Neck, a near-island.

Matchapunko (Herrman map) (1670)

Neck: Accomack County; near the Machipungo Indian town; probably Upshur or Bell Neck.

Matchapungo (PB 5:348) (1664)

Place: King and Queen County; on the Mattaponi River's left bank; near Garretts Creek.

Matchepungo (PB 3:30) (1653)

Place: Middlesex (formerly Lancaster) County; on the Rappahannock River's right bank; in the vicinity of the Piankatank River's upper reaches; probably near Matchapungo Creek and Urbanna.

Matchapungo (PB 5:226) (1663)

River: Accomack and Northampton Counties; a tributary of the Great Machipongo Channel, which flows into the Atlantic Ocean.
Matchepungo (PB 2:134) (1647)
Matchepongo (PB 3:247) (1653)
Mathepungo (PB 5:186) (1664)
Machepungo (PB 5:377) (1664)
Matsepunge (PB 6:306) (1670)
Matsihapunko (Herrman map) (1670)
Matchapongo (PB 6:540) (1674)
Matchepungo (Northampton County Orders, Wills 1674-1679:312) (1678)
Mattchepungo (Northampton County Wills, Deeds, etc. 1711-1718:125) (1716)

Sandbar: Accomack and Northampton Counties; parallels the Atlantic coast.

Matsihapunck (Herrman map) (1670)

MACHODOC

Creek and River (Lower): Westmoreland County (formerly Northumberland); a tributary on the Potomac River's right side; the east side of Machodoc Neck and the west side of Coles Neck.

Mackatix (PB 2:247) (1650)
Machotick (PB 2:250) (1650)
Matchoux (PB 2:273) (1650)
Mattchotick (PB 2:280) (1650)
Matchotiq (PB 2:287) (1650)
Mackotick (PB 3:38) (1653)
Matchoticke (PB 3:72) (1653)
Matchotique (PB 3:220) (1653)
Matchotix (PB 3:277) (1654)
Match Choaticke (PB 4:86) (1656)
Machoatick (PB 4:126) (1657)
Machotix (PB 4:182) (1657)
Mechoticks (PB 4:314) (1661)
Machoticque (PB 4:323) (1661)
Machotique (PB 4:90) (1662)
Machotanck (Northumberland County Record Book 1662-1666:129) (1664)
Machoatick (PB 4:111) (1664)
Machoticke (PB 5:393) (1664)
Natchosiq (PB 5:425) (1665)
Machotigue (PB 5:431) (1665)

Powhatan Indian Place Names in Tidewater Virginia

Mattschotick (Herrman map) (1670)
Machotocke (PB 6:691) (1679)
Machotic (Warner map) (1736-1737)
Machotick (Jefferson-Brooke map) (1747)
Machodock (Fry-Jefferson map) (1751)
Matchodock (Henry map) (1770)
Machodoc (Tatham map) (1813)

Creek and River (Upper): King George (formerly Westmoreland) County; a tributary on the Potomac River's right side; near Dahlgren; also known as the Trent River.

Machotiq (PB 2:275) (1650)
Machoatick (Northumberland County Record Book 1658-1662:39) (1650)
Mattchotiq (PB 2:301) (1651)
Mattchotiqs (PB 2:354) (1651)
Machotake (Northumberland County Wills and Inventories 1652-1658:2)(1651)
Mucholix (Westmoreland County Deeds, Wills, Patents &c 1653-1659:22) (1652)
Matchotique (PB 3:70) (1653)
Matchotix (PB 3:374) (1654)
Matchoticke (PB 4:57) (1656)
Machaotick (Northumberland County Wills, Inventories &c. 1652-1658:101) (1656)
Machoatick (PB 4:201) (1657)
Muttchotick (Westmoreland County Deeds, Wills &c 1661-1662:6-6a) (1660)
Machoticks (PB 4:307) (1661)
Machotike (PB 6:179) (1661)
Machtiack (Northumberland County Record Book 1666-1670: 34-36) (1667)
Machodick (Westmoreland County, Deeds and Wills 1:198) (1662)
Machotick (PB 5:170) (1662)
Machoatique (Northumberland County Record Book 1662-1666:96) (1663)
Mattschotick (Herrman map) (1670)
Mechotick (PB 6:363) (1671)

Majotock (Richmond County Deed Book 2 [1693-1695]:152-157) (1694)
Machotick (Warner map) (1736-1737)
Mahotack (Jefferson-Brooke map) (1747)
Matchodock (Henry map) (1770)
Machodoc (Anonymous map) (1776)
Machodock (Tatham map) (1813)

Indian Town: King George (formerly Northumberland and Westmoreland) County; on both sides of Upper Machodoc Creek. In 1657, the chief's name was Pertatoan, and two years later one of his tribesmen was named George Casquesough (PP 122).

Muchchotas (Northumberland County Deeds and Orders 1650-1652:50) (1650)
Upper Mattchotiqs (PB 2:354) (1651)
Muchchotas (Northumberland County, Deeds and Orders 1650-1652: 50) (1651)
Upper Mucholox (Westmoreland County Deeds, Wills, Patents &c 1653-1659:22) (1652)
Matchotwick (PB 3:273) (1654)
Machoatick (Northumberland County Wills, Inventories &c. 1652-1658:94) (1656)
Upper Machotick (PB 4:201) (1657)
Machoticke (PB 4:80) (1662)
Upper Machotix (PB 5:296) (1662)
Machoatick (Northumberland County Record Book 1662-1666:124) (1663)

Indian Towns: Caroline and King George Counties; on both sides of the Rappahannock River; in the vicinity of Portobago Bay and the Nanzattico town of 1669 (see Mattehatique).

Neck: King George County; on the Potomac River's right bank; west of Upper Machodoc Creek; probably Mathias Neck or Point.

Powhatan Indian Place Names in Tidewater Virginia

Mattchotick (PB 2:285) (1650)
Machoticke (PB 3:14) (1653)

Neck: Westmoreland County; on the Potomac River's right bank; a neck of land bound on the east by Lower Machodoc Creek and on the west by Nomini Creek.

Mattchotick (PB 2:285) (1650)
Machoticke (PB 3:14) (1653)

Parish: Westmoreland County; formed from part of Nomini Parish around 1653-1654 and named for "Machodick" Creek; became extinct in 1664 (DVA 166-167).

Path: Lancaster, Northumberland, Richmond, and Westmoreland Counties; a trail that traversed the Northern Neck, in its eastward extent passing close to both Totuskey Creek and the Great Wicomoco River.

Ma Choticke (PB 4:102) (1662)
Machoticke (PB 4:102) (1662)
Machoticks (PB 4:279) (1662)
Machotick (PB 4:296) (1662)
Machotickes (PB 4:300) (1662)
Machoticke (Lancaster County Deeds and Wills 1661-1672:372) (1662)
Machotick (Northumberland County Record Book 1666-1670:117-118) (1670)

Place: Northumberland County; on the Potomac River's right bank; near Machodoc Creek.

Little Mechotick (Northumberland County Record Book 1666-1670: 67) (1668)

MACHOTANK

Place: Northampton County; in the vicinity of Onancock Creek (PB 4:458) (1660)

MACKATOUSES

Creek: Northampton County; a tributary of Nassawadox Creek.

Mackatouses (Accomack County, Deeds and Wills 1663-1666:76) (1664)

MACKSOOMUCK

Neck: Northampton County; one of several necks of land formed by Nassawadox Creek.

Macksoomuck (PB 4:461) (1660)

MAGOTHY

Bay: Northampton County; a tributary of Atlantic Ocean that runs between Mockhorn Island and the mainland.

Maggitye (PB 1:322) (1635)
Magatie (PB 1:366) (1636)
Magaty (PB 1:416) (1637)
Maggetye (PB 1:817) (1642)
Maggetty (PB 2:365) (1643)
Magetty (PB 4:32) (1656)
Maggatte (Northampton County Deeds, Wills, Etc. 1655-1657:22) (1656)
Magattbay (Northampton County Deeds, Wills, Etc. 1657-1666:30) (1658)
Magette (PB 6:83) (1667)
Maggettibay (Northampton County Deeds, Wills, Etc. 1666-1668:17) (1667)
Maggative (Northampton County Deeds, Wills, Etc. 1680-1692:42) (1679)

Powhatan Indian Place Names in Tidewater Virginia

Maggotty (Northampton County Orders, Wills, Etc. 1683-1689:339) (1688)
Magete (Northampton County Wills, Deeds, etc. 1711-1718:40) (1712)
Maggoty (Northampton County Wills and Inventories, 1733-1740:285) (1732)
Magotty (Northampton County Wills and Inventories 1750-1754:325) (1751)

MAMA SHEEMENT

Place: King and Queen or Essex (formerly New Kent) County; on the left side of the Mattaponi River, probably along the low ridge separating the Mattaponi and Rappahannock River valleys.

Mama Sheement (PB 3:345) (1655)

MAMANAHUNT

Indian Town: Charles City County; on the Chickahominy River's right bank; near Wilcox Neck.

Mattalunt (CJS I:41) (1608)
Mamanahunt (CJS I:42) (1608)
Mamanakunt (Smith map) (1612)
Manahunt (Ogilby map) (1676)

MAMANASSY

Indian Town: King and Queen County; on the Mattaponi River's left bank; at or near Brookshire.

Mamanast (Zuniga map) (1608)
Mamanassi (Velasco map) (1610)
Mamanassy (Smith map) (1612)
Mamanassa (Ogilby map) (1676)

MANAGIRACK

Path: Westmoreland County; a trail near Popes Creek.

Managirack (PB 5:277) (1663)
Mangiarick (Westmoreland County, Deeds and Wills 1:250) (1664)

MANAKIN

Creek: Powhatan (formerly Henrico) County; a tributary on the James River's right side. Derived from the name of the Siouan-speaking Monacan Indians, the Powhatans' enemy. The Monacans' name for themselves was not recorded.

Manakin (PB 9:437) (1702)

Place: Goochland (formerly Henrico) County; the site of a French Huguenot settlement on the James River's left bank, near Sabot Island; originally site of the Monacan Indians' town, Mowhemchco.

Monakin (Lederer map) (1670)
Manakin Town (Fry-Jefferson map) (1751)
Manakin (Captaine map) (1781)

MANGA KEMOXON

Indian Town: King George County; on the Rappahannock River's left bank near Port Conway; a portion of the Nansemond Indian town.

Mange-Communkson (Old Rappahannock County Deeds, Wills, Inventories &c 1656-1664:357) (1664)
Mangecomupon (Old Rappahannock County Deeds, Wills, Inventories, &c 1668-1672:228) (1670)
Nangimocxen (Herrman map) (1670)
Manga Kemoxon (Old Rappahannock

Powhatan Indian Place Names in Tidewater Virginia

County Deeds Wills, Inventories, &c 1677-1687:64) (1678)

MANGOHICK

Creek: King William County; a tributary on the Pamunkey River's left side; now known as Millpond Creek. The name is still preserved in a crossroads settlement in the county.

Mangohick Creek (PB 9:562) (1703)
Mangohick (William Byrd Title Book 215) ([1712])
Mangehick (PB 10:87) (1713)
Mongohick (PB 9:58) (1724)
Mangohick (Boye map) (1826)

MANGORACA

Indian Town: Westmoreland County; on the Rappahannock River's left bank; above Brockenbrough Creek and near Smith Mount Landing.

Mangoraca (Smith map) (1612)

MANGORICK

Place: Richmond County; on the Rappahannock River left bank; between Totuskey and Farnham Creeks.

Mangorick (Old Rappahannock County Deeds, Wills, Inventories &c 1656-1664:39) (1658)

MANGORIGHT

Point: Richmond County; on the Rappahannock River's left bank; near McGuire Creek and opposite modern Tappahannock.

Mangoright (USGS Tappahannock quadrangle) (1917)

MANIMASS

Creek: City of Chesapeake (formerly Norfolk County); a tributary of Deep Creek, which flows into the Elizabeth River's South Branch.

Manimass (PB 5:191) (1663)

MANNAHORRADONS

Neck: Northampton County; a neck of land, perhaps near Nandua Creek.

Mannahorradons (Northampton County Deeds, Wills, Etc. 1657-1666:149) (1663)
Monhorridom (Northampton County Wills, Deeds, etc. 1711-1718:40) (1712)

MANOAKIN

Place: Accomack County; probably near Gargaphy Neck.

Manoakin (PB 5:191) (1664).

River: Accomack County; adjacent to Gargaphy Neck; probably Gargaphy Creek, a tributary of Gargaphy Bay.

Manoakin (PB 5:191) (1664).

MANQUIN

Creek and Swamp: King William County; a tributary on the Pamunkey River's left side; present Moncuin Creek. The "Manquin" spelling remains in the name of a settlement nearby, along U.S. 360.

Monkewin Swamp (PB 9:78) (1695)

Powhatan Indian Place Names in Tidewater Virginia

Muquer (Fry-Jefferson map) (1751)
Muquen (Captaine map) (1781)
Maquer (Madison map) (1807)
Moncuin (Boye map) (1826)

MANSA

Indian Town: Charles City County; on the Chickahominy River's right bank; on Old Neck, between Sunken Marsh and Mount Airy.

Mansa (Zuniga map) (1608)
Mansa (CJS I:41) (1608)

MANSKIN

Fort: King William County; on the Pamunkey River's left bank; above Moncuin Creek; site of Fort Royall, a surveillance post and trade center established by the English in 1645.

The Indian Fort (Langston map) (1662)
Manaskin (PB 5:370) (1664)

Indian Town: King William County; on the Pamunkey River's left bank.

Manaskunt (Zuniga map) (1608)

Indian Town: King William County; on the Pamunkey River's left bank; near Moncuin Creek.

Manskin Indian (Herrman map) (1670)

Place: King William County; on the Pamunkey River's left banknear Moncuin Creek; opposite Totopotomoy Creek's mouth.

Manskin (PB 6:19) (1666)

MANSOTANZIC

Creek: Northampton County; a tributary on the Nassawadox Creek's left side; possibly Holly Grove Cove.

Mansotanzick (PB 2:184) (1649)
Mossacotanzick (PB 2:185) (1649)
Mussatanzick (PB 6:372) (1671)

MANTAPIKE

Creek: King and Queen County; a tributary on the Mattaponi River's left side; possible site of an Indian ferry.

Mantapike (Fry-Jefferson map) (1751)

Place: King and Queen County; on the Mattaponi River's left bank; downstream from Mantapike Creek.

Mantpoyick (PB 3:32) (1653)
Mantapike (Herrman map) (1670)
Mantipike (PB 8:36) (1690)

Place: Spotsylvania or Stafford County; at the falls of the Rappahannock River.

Mantepeuck (LED 34) (1672)

MANTOUGHQUEMEC

Indian Town: City of Suffolk (formerly Nansemond County); on the Nansemond River's right bank; probably upstream from the mouth of the Western Branch, in the vicinity of Wilroy.

Mantoughquemec (Smith map) (1612)
Mantoughquemend (Ogilby map) (1676)

MANTUA

Ferry: King William County; on the

Powhatan Indian Place Names in Tidewater Virginia

Mattaponi River's right bank; above White Oak Landing.

Mantua (Gilmer 1864a)

MAPSICO

Creek: Charles City County; a tributary of Kittawan Creek, itself a tributary on the James River's left side.

Matticoe (PB 1:206) (1635)
Matchocoes (PB 1:295) (1635)
Matshcoes (PB 2:266) (1650)
Mapscoe (PB 6:265) (1671)
Match Coates (PB 10:42) (1711)

Place: New Kent County; deed to William Bassett from Lewis Burwell.

Matchcoake (Bassett Family Papers) (1668)

MARACOSSIC

Creek and Swamp: King and Queen and Caroline Counties; a tributary of Beverley Creek, itself a tributary on the Mattaponi River's left side.

Morocosick (PB 8:131) (1691)
Morocosick Creek (PB 9:721) (1706)
Maracosick Swamp (PB 10:94) (1713)
Marracosack (Fry-Jefferson map) (1751)

MARRACOONES

Creek: City of Suffolk (formerly Nansemond County); probably on the western edge of the Great Dismal Swamp.

Marracoones (PB 4:9) (1655)
Marrocone (PB 4:63) (1656)

MARTOUGHQUAUNK

Indian Town: King and Queen County; on the Mattaponi River's left bank, just above Walkerton.

Mateughguaent (Zuniga map) 1608)
Martoughquaunk (Smith map) (1612)

MARUMSCO

Creek: Prince William County; a tributary of Occoquan Bay; probably Powells Creek.

Morumscoe (NN 1:150) (1692)

MASSACOON

Creek: Richmond County; a tributary on the Rappahannock River's left side in its freshwater reaches.

Massacoon (Richmond County Deed Book 2 [1693-1695]:198-199) (1696)

MASSAPONAX

Creek, Run, and Swamp: Spotsylvania (formerly Essex) County; a tributary on the Rappahannock River's right side; below Fredericksburg and near New Post.

Nusaponucks (PB 5:481) (1666)
Nusaponocks (PB 6:356) (1671)
Nussaponocks (PB 6:410) (1672)
Nussaponaxe (PB 6:491) (1673)
Nasaponnecks (PB 7:198) (1682)
Nusapommacks (PB 7:292) (1683)
Nussaponox (PB 10:322) (1717)
Messaponax (PB 10:407) (1718)
Messaponnax (PB 10:407) (1718)
Nussaponock (PB 9:58) (1720)
Nussaponax (PB 13:354) (1729)

Powhatan Indian Place Names in Tidewater Virginia

Nassaponock (PB 14:54) (1730)
Massaponax (Fry-Jefferson map) 1751)
Maseponax (Henry map) (1770)
Massaponax (Captaine map) (1781)

MASSAWOTECK

Indian Town: King George County; on the Rappahannock River's left bank; across from the upstream side of Moss Neck.

Massawoteck (Smith map) (1612)
Massawteck (CJS III:174) (1624)

MASSINACACH

Indian Town: Powhatan County; on the James River's right bank; near Michaux and below the Route 522 bridge; a king's house. This probably was a Siouan-speaking Monacan name, rather than an Algonquian-speaking Powhatan one.

Monahassanugh (Zuniga map) (1608)
Massinacach (Smith map) (1612)
Masinacatk (Vingboons map) (1639)

MASSIPONEY

Creek: Richmond (formerly King George) County; somewhere north of the Rappahannock River; possibly near the place called Mattapony (q.v.), near Dahlgren.

Massiponey (Richmond County Deed Book 2 [1693-1695]:11-12) (1691)

MATACHEPENECK

Creek: Northampton County; a tributary on Occohannock Creek's right side.

Matachepeneck (PB 4:25) (1655)

MATADEQUIN

Creek: boundary between New Kent and Hanover Counties; a tributary on the Pamunkey River's right side.

Moggadegum (PB 2:201) (1649)
Mattadequain (PB 2:313) (1651)
Mackadequin (PB 3:370) (1653)
Mattedecum (PB 4:299) (1662)
Mattuttaquid (Langston map) (1662)
Mattedecon (PB 5:267) (1663)
Matterdam (PB 5:357) (1663)
Mattadecum (PB 5:503) (1666)
Mattadekon (PB 6:150) (1668)
Mattadequne (PB 6:213) (1668)
Mattadequn (PB 6:302) (1670)
Mattadqun (PB 6:464) (1673)
Madadecums (PB 6:536) (1674)
Mattedequin (PB 6:680) (1679)
Matte De Quin (PB 7:85) (1681)
Mattadequm (PB 7:115) (1681)
Matadequnn (PB 7:658) (1688)
Mattadecun (PB 8:129) (1691)
Mataducun (PB 12:432) (1725)
Metadequan (Fry-Jefferson map) (1751)
Metadequan (Henry map) (1770)
Matadequin (Captaine map) (1781)
Matedyqueen (Hanover County Deed Book 1783-1792:504) (1791)
Meladquin (Anonymous map) (1878)

Creek: King William County; a tributary on the Pamunkey River's left; now known as Herrick Creek and Olssons Pond.

Tanks Maccadequin (PB 2:226) (1650)
Tancks Maccadegums (PB 3:93) (1652)
Tanckes Maddaqume (PB 3:34) (1653)
Tanckes Maddaquine (PB 3:34) (1653)
Tanx Mattadaquain (PB 3:34) (1653)
Tanx Mattadaquin (PB 3:34) (1653)

Powhatan Indian Place Names in Tidewater Virginia

Tanks Mattedequin (PB 3:291) 1653)

Path: New Kent County; a trail running west from Weyanock (now Cattail) Swamp, near the Pamunkey River, and crossing Matadequin Creek.

Maddicon (PB 4:324) (1662)

Run: New Kent County; a branch of Diascund (or Tyascan) Swamp.

Mattadequince Run (PB 9:704) (1705)

MATAHUNK

Neck: Charles City County; on the Chickahominy River's right bank; between Tonyham and Dockman Swamps.

Mattahunck (PB 1:640) (1639)
Mattahauck (PB 1:640) (1639)
Mattahuncke (PB 1:668) (1639)
Mattahunke (PB 1:812) (1642)
Mattahuncks (PB 4:256) (1658)
Mattahancks (PB 5:332) (1663)
Matahunk (Patterson map) (1873-1874)

MATCHEMAPPS

Branch: Lancaster County; at the head of Morattico Creek.

Matchemapps (PB 3:235) (1653)

MATCHOPICK

Indian Town: Richmond County; on the Rappahannock River's left bank; downriver from the mouth of Brockenborough Creek, in the vicinity of Luke's Island.

Matchopick (Smith map) (1612)

Matchopeak (CJS III:174) (1624)

MATCHOTANK

Creek: Accomack County; a tributary of Chesapeake Bay; south of Onancock Creek.

Matchotank (PB 3:244) (1653)
Matchotanke (PB 4:9) (1655)
Little Anancocke (PB 4:9) (1655)
Matchatank (PB 7:589) (1687)
Matchatank (Boye map) (1826)

Place: Accomack County; area near Machotank Creek.

Matchotanke (PB 3:106) (1652)
Matchotanck (PB 6:423) (1661)

MATCHUT

Indian Town: New Kent County; on the Pamunkey River's right bank, near Eltham Marsh.

Mattchamins (Zuniga map) (1608)
Matchut (Smith map) (1612)
Matchot (CJS II:245) (1612)
Muskunt (CJS II:245) (1612)
Matchcot (HAILE 807) (1614)
Matehut (Ogilby map) (1676)

MATCHUTT

Indian Town: King and Queen County; on the Mattaponi River's left bank, between the mouths of Heartquake and Old Mill Creeks.

Matchutt (Smith map) (1612)
Matchutt (Ogilby map) (1676)

MATCHYCOMICOE

Branch: Richmond County; near

47

Powhatan Indian Place Names in Tidewater Virginia

Totuskey Creek.

Matchacomac (Richmond County Deed Book 1 [1692-1693]:134-137) (1691)
Matchycomicoe (Richmond County Deed Book 2:1693-1695]:130-133) (1695)

Place: Stafford County; location at which Indians met to hold a council or parley (HEN II:194).

Machacomoca (Stafford County Record Book 1686-1693:236a) (1692)

MATHOMAUK

Indian Town: Isle of Wight County; on the James River's right bank; between Tormentor Creek and Burwell Bay.

Mattanock (Velasco map) (1610)
Mathomauk (Smith map) (1612)
Mathomauk (Ogilby map) (1676)

MATSAPREAK

Creek and Inlet: Accomack County; modern Folly Creek and Cedar Island and Metomkin Inlets, above Cedar (formerly Teaches) Island; on the seaside.

Matampken (Herrman map) (1670)
Matsapreak (Fry-Jefferson map) (1751)
Mataspreak (Henry map) (1770)

MATSIHAPUNCK

Shoals: Northampton County; on the seaside, north of Mockhorn Island.

Matsihapunck (Herrman map) (1670)
Matsihapuncko (Thornton-Fisher map) (1698-1705)

MATTACOCK

Creek and Swamp: King William (formerly King and Queen) County; a tributary on the Pamunkey River's left side, near Cohoke Creek.

Mastico (PB 9:434) (1702)
Masticock Swamp (PB 9:655) (1705)

Indian Town: Gloucester County; on the York River's left bank; on the east side of Adams Creek.

Mattacock (Smith map) (1612)

MATTACOCY

Branch and Creek: King and Queen County; a tributary of the Mattaponi River not far from its division into three forks, the Matta, Po, and Ni Rivers.

Mattacocy (Boye map) (1826)

MATTACUNT

Indian Town: King George County; on the Potomac Creek's right bank; near Bull Bluff.

Mattacunt (Smith map) (1612)

MATTANOCK

Indian Town: City of Suffolk (formerly Nansemond County); on the Nansemond River's left bank; across from Glebe Point; upstream from Cedar Creek.

Mattanock (Smith map) (1612)

Powhatan Indian Place Names in Tidewater Virginia

MATTAPONI

Creek: Gloucester County; a tributary on the York River's left side; downstream from PoropotankRiver; present Adams Creek.

Mattopony (PB 3:52) (1653)

Creek or Run: King and Queen and Essex Counties; a tributary of Dragon Swamp.

Mattopany (PB 9:214) (1699)

Creek: Accomack County; in the vicinity of Swans Gut and Coldkall Creeks.

Mattapony (Accomack County Wills and Deeds 1676-1690:19) (1677)

Fort: King and Queen County; on the Mattaponi River's left bank at Newington, near Locust Grove and to the east of Walkerton. For reasons that are unclear, in 1653 Edward Diggs' patent in this vicinity was known as the "Matapony Fort." In 1679 a fortified outpost was built by the Virginia government on Jacob Lumpkin's land "at or above the Indian towns." This garrison, called the "Mattapony Fort," was erected in the aftermath of Bacon's Rebellion.

Matapony Fort (PB 3:16) (1653)
Mattapony Fort (HEN II:434) (1679)

Indian Ferry: King William and King and Queen Counties; between Gleasons Marsh and Davis Beach, adjacent to Georges Swamp.

Mattapony (PB 3:4) (1653)

Indian Reservation: King William County; on the Mattaponi River's right bank; adjacent to Indian Town Swamp; upstream from Wakema.

Indian Town: James City County; on Chickahominy River's right bank, probably between Yarmouth Creek and Uncles Neck.

Matapamient (CJS I: 41) (1608)
Mattapanient (Zuniga map) (1608)
Matapament (Smith map) (1612)

Indian Town: King and Queen County; located on a tributary on the Mattaponi River's left side; formerly known as Hashwamankcott Swamp or Branch; now called Garnetts Creek.

Matopony (PB 6:425) (1672)

Indian Town: King and Queen and/or Essex County; attacked by the Seneca Indians.

Mattapony (EJC I:53) (1683)

Indian Town: King and Queen and/or Essex (formerly New Kent and/or Old Rappahannock) County; in the headwaters of modern Piscataway Creek, on the ridge between the Mattaponi and Rappahannock River valleys.

Mattapony (PB 4:77) (1662)
Mattapany (Old Rappahannock County Deed Book 3:425-426) (1668)
Pattipany (Old Rappahannock Record Book 1672-1676:7-8) (1671)
Matopony (PB 6:425) (1672)

Indian Tribe: King William and King and Queen Counties; traditionally

Powhatan Indian Place Names in Tidewater Virginia

located along both sides of the Mattaponi River. In ca. 1610, Werowough was the chief of this territory (HAILE 628).

Matapoll (HAILE 117) (1607)
Mattapamient (CJS II:256) (1612)
Mattapanient (Haile 628) (1612)

Indian Tribe: King and Queen (formerly New Kent) County. When a census of the native population was taken in 1669, the Mattaponi were described as residents of New Kent County. The Mattaponi Indians' town was located in the headwaters of modern Piscataway Creek, on the ridge between the Mattaponi and Rappahannock River valleys. In 1656 the tribe's chief was Tupeisens, and his councilors were Owmohowtne, Mennenhcom, Eriopochke, and Peponngeis (PP114n.).

Mattapanies (HEN II:275) (1669)

Neck: James City County; on the Chickahominy Rivers right bank, adjacent to Rickahock Creek. probably site of the village Captain John Smith identified as Matapamient in 1608.

Mattapony (PB 4:55) (1656)
Mettopony (PB 4:175) (1658)
Mattaponnigh (Isle of Wight County Wills and Deeds 1:24) (1664)

Neck: Accomack (formerly Northampton) County; between Swans Gut and Coldkall Creeks, tributaries of Chincoteague Bay; now known as Winders Neck.

Matapanie (Northampton County, Deeds and Wills 1657-1666:44) (1657)
Matapany (Accomack County, Orders and Wills 1671-1673: 75) (1672)
Mattapenny (Accomack County, Orders and Wills 1671-1673: 126) (1672)

Path: Essex, Gloucester, and Middlesex Counties; a two-pronged path that emanated from the post-1644 Mattaponi Indian town in King and Queen/Essex County. The right path ran along the head of Porotpotank River in Gloucester County; the left path paralleled the Piankatank River and Dragon Run, touching the heads of Nimcock Creek in Middlesex County and Occupacia Creek in Essex County.

Mattapony (PB 2:338) (1651)
Mattapony (Lancaster County Deeds and Wills 1661-1672:249-250) (1662)
Mattopony (PB 5:199) (1663)

Place: Accomack County; location on the Swans Gut Creek's right bank close to the Maryland line and on the seaside.

Mattapony (PB 6:32) (1666)
Mattapany (PB 6:32) (1666)
Matappany (PB 6:34) (1666)

Place: King George County; on Upper Machodoc Creek's left bank, near present Dahlgren.

Mattpony (Westmoreland County, Deeds and Wills 1:198) (1662)
Metaponie (Northumberland County Record Book 1662-1666:146) (1664)

Place: James City County; on the left bank of the Chickahominy River near Rickahock.

Mattopeneigh (Isle of Wight County Will and Deed Book 1 [1662-1688]:24) (1664)

Powhatan Indian Place Names in Tidewater Virginia

Mattapeneigh (Isle of Wight County Will and Deed Book 1 [1662-1688]:24) (1664)

River: boundary between King William and King and Queen Counties; a tributary on the York River's left side.

Mattapanient (CJS I:51) (1608)
Mattapanyent (CJS III:317) (1624)
Mattapony (PB 1:926) (1643)
Matapony (PB 2:108) (1647)
Mettonpony (PB 4:166) (1652)
Mettapony (PB 3:213) (1653)
Metopony (PB 3:217) (1653)
Mettopony (PB 3:291) (1653)
Mattepony (PB 4:48) (1656)
Mettepony (PB 4:101) (1657)
Mattopany (PB 4:183) (1658)
Mattapany (PB 4:184) (1658)
Metapony (PB 5:337) (1662)
Matapoine (Langston map) (1662)
Mattopony (PB 5:216) (1663)
Mattaponie (PB 6:70) (1666)
Mattapiony (PB 6:299) (1670)
Mattapainy (PB 6:302) (1670)
Matapeneugh (LED 1958:16) (1672)
Metapeneu (LED map) (1672)
Mattapony (Fry-Jefferson map) (1751)
Matapony (Seib map) (1858)

River: Northumberland County; on the South Branch of the Yeocomico River; probably associated with Lodge Creek.

Mattapony (PB 3:12) (1653)
Mettopony (PB 3:329) (1654)
Matapony (PB 4:39) (1656)
Mattapany (PB 4:196) (1657)
Mattaponie (PB 6:70) (1666)
Matoponey (Northumberland County Record Book 1666-1670:1) (1666)

MATTAQUINCE

Swamp: James City County; a tributary of Diascund Creek (which is a tributary on the Chickahominy River's left side), near a meadow and a branch with a spring.

Marraquince (PB 5:153) (1664)
Mattaquince (PB 5:342) (1664)

MATTASACK

Creek: King and Queen (formerly New Kent) County; a tributary on the York River's left side; in the vicinity of Goalders Creek.

Mattasack (PB 6:91) (1666)

MATTASIP

Neck: Northampton County; somewhere near Occohannock Creek.

Mattasip (PB 2:76) (1647)
Matasippy Neck (Northampton County Deeds, Wills, Etc. 1657-1666:27) (1658)
Mattiaippe Neck (Northampton County Deeds, Wills, Etc. 1708-1717:4) (1708)
Matysipy (Northampton County Wills and Inventories 1733-1740:288) (1738)

Place: Northampton County; an English plantation.

Mattinaippe (Northampton County Deeds, Wills, Etc. 1708-1717:4) (1708)

MATTASUP

Swamp: King and Queen County; on the left side of the Mattaponi River; near the site of Stratton Major Parish Church.

Powhatan Indian Place Names in Tidewater Virginia

Montassup (PB 4:253) (1658)
Montesup (PB 4:257) (1658)
Mattasup (PB 4:318) (1662)
Mattasux (PB 4:309) (1662)
Mattassop (PB 7:592) (1687)
Mattassup (PB 9:556) (1703)

MATTAWOMAN

Creek: Northampton County; a tributary of the Chesapeake Bay; adjoining and just below Hungars Creek.

Mattawomens (PB 1:244) (1635)
Mattawambs (PB 3:286) (1653)
Matawoms (PB 6:256) (1664)
Mattawoms (PB 6:439) (1672)
Mattowoames (Northampton County Orders 1679-1683:287) (1682)
Mattawomes (Northampton County Orders, Wills, Etc. 1683-1689:102) (1684)
Mattawoms (Northampton County Orders, Wills, Etc. 1689-1698:419) (1695)
Mattawama (Northampton County Wills, Deeds, etc. 1711-1718:144) (1718)
Mattawoman (Northampton County Wills, Deeds, Etc. 1718-1725:78) (1720)

Indian Town: Northampton County; probably near Mattawoman Creek, a tributary of the Chesapeake Bay.

Mattawombes (HEN I: 167) (1632)

MATTAWOMPSON

Creek: Northampton County; a tributary on the left side of Nassawadox Creek, which in turn is a tributary of the Chesapeake Bay.

Mattawompson (PB 2:185) (1649)

Mattawamson (Northampton County Orders, Deeds, and Wills 4 [1651-1654]:154) (1653)

MATTEHATIQUE

Indian Towns: Caroline and King George (formerly Old Rappahannock) Counties; in the vicinity of Portobago Bay and the Nanzattico Indian town, on one or both sides of the Rappahannock River. In 1669 the Mattehatique Indians were living close to the Nanzattico and Portobago tribes and may have been the Machodoc (formerly Onawmanient) people. A silver badge that belonged to the King of Machotick was found at Camden farm on Portobago Bay in Caroline County.

Mattehatique (HEN II:275) (1669)

MATTOAX

Place: Chesterfield County; on the Appomattox River's left bank, above the falls and approximately a mile from Petersburg. The name, very similar to Pocahontas's real name, is reflected in that of a mid-19th century community that grew up around the Matoaca Mills.

Matoaca (Gilmer map) (1863)
Mattoax (LaPrade map) (1880)

MATTOONES

Creek: King and Queen (formerly Gloucester) County; a tributary on the Mattaponi River's left side; probably downstream from Mantapike Creek.

Mattoones (PB 3:32) (1653)

Powhatan Indian Place Names in Tidewater Virginia

Creek and Sunken Ground: New Kent County; a tributary on the Pamunkey River right side.

Mattoone (PB 7:225) (1682)

Indian Town: Northampton County; near Hungars Creek; a probable misspelling of Mattawoman.
Mattoones (PB 1:507) (1637)

MATTUM SARKIN

Place: Essex County; on the Rappahannock River's right bank near an island; in the vicinity of Quioccasin Creek, which is the head of Broad Creek.

Mattum Sarkin (PB 3:1) (1653)
Mattumsarkin (PB 4:304) (1663)

MATUNSK

Indian Town: Hanover County; on the Pamunkey River's right bank, above Whiting Swamp's mouth.

Matunsk (Zuniga map) (1608)

MAUKES, THE GREAT

Place: Prince George County; trees near head of Powells Creek and the Weyanock Indians' Old Town.

The Great Maukes (PB 2:248) (1650)

MAZAPIN

Swamp: Essex County; location on the Rappahannock River's right side.

Mazapin (Essex County Deeds and Wills 1699-1702:15) (1665)

MAZINOAOS

Indian Town: James City County; on the Chickahominy River's left bank; below Yarmouth Creek.

Mazinoaos (Zuniga map) (1608)

MECHUMPS

Creek: Hanover County; a tributary of Campbell Creek, itself a tributary on the Pamunkey River's right side; the creek's headwaters are in Ashland.

Matchump (PB 7:556) (1687)
Mathumps (PB 8:103) (1690)
Machumps (PB 8:105) (1690)
Michunck (PB 14:396) (1732)
Machunck Creek (PB 14:396) (1732)
Mechums (Fry-Jefferson map) (1751)
Mechumps (Henry map) (1770)

MEHIXEN

Branch and Creek: New Kent and Hanover Counties; a branch of Totopotomoy Creek, itself a tributary of the Pamunkey River's right side.

Mohixen (PB 5:416) (1665)
Mehixon (Boye map) 1826)

Creek: King William (formerly King and Queen) County; on the Pamunkey River's left side; it joins with Sullens Creek and two other tributaries and flows into the Pamunkey's left side.

Mahixon (PB 9:368) (1701)
Matuxen Creek (PB 12:249) (1725)
Mehixon (Fry-Jefferson map) (1751)

Powhatan Indian Place Names in Tidewater Virginia

Fort: King William County; located on the left side of the Pamunkey River, probably near the creek of the same name; site of a fort the Virginia government built in March 1676 as a defense against the Indians.

Mehixon Fort (HEN II:328)

Place: New Kent County; on the Pamunkey River's right bank; above Totopotomoy Creek's mouth.

Mahexem (PB 6:290) (1670)
Matrexem (PB 6:290) (1670)
Mahixeen (PB 6:301) (1670)
Mahaxeenes (PB 6:504) (1673)
Mehixon (PB 8:163) (1691)

MENASCOSIC

Indian Town: Charles City County; on the Chickahominy River's right bank, across from Diascund Creek's mouth.

Manosquosick (CJS I:39) (1608)
Maraqusic (Zuniga map) (1608)
Menascosic (Smith map) (1612)

MENAPUCUNT

Indian Town: King William County; on the Pamunkey River's left bank, just above Lee Marsh. In ca. 1610, Ottondeacommoc was the chief of this town (HAILE 628).

Manapacunt (Zuniga map, 1608)
Menapacute (CJS I:51) (1608)
Menapacant (CJS I:77) (1608)
Menapucunt (Smith map) (1612)
Mummapacun (HAILE 628) (1612)

MENASKUNT

Indian Town: Richmond County; on the Rappahannock River's left bank; west of Totoskey Creek.

Menaskunt (Smith map) (1612)

MENCOCOCOND, NEW

River: Richmond County; a tributary on the Rappahannock River's left side; below Farnham Creek; possibly same as Morrattico Creek.

New Mencococond (PB 2:230) (1650)

MENCUGHTAS

Indian Town: Hanover County; on the Pamunkey River's right bank, near the mouth of Crump Creek.

Mencughtas (Zuniga map) (1608)

MENENASK

Indian Town: King George County; on the Rappahannock River's left bank, near Cleve.

Menenask (Smith map) (1612)

MENMEND

Creek: Hanover County; a tributary on the Pamunkey River's right side, across from Menmend or The Island; by 1672 the creek had become known as Totopotomoy Creek.

Menmend (Langston map) (1662)

Indian Town: King William County; large island in the Pamunkey River near

Powhatan Indian Place Names in Tidewater Virginia

Carter's Landing and east of Moncuin (formerly Manquin) Creek; now known as The Island; probably the same as Warranucock Island. Cartographer Anthony Langston indicated that the island was "an ancient seat of Opachancone [Opechancanough] ye late Emperour" or paramount chief.

Menmend (Langston map) (1662)

MENOKIN

Bay, Run, and Swamp: Richmond County; the name is now applied only to the bay, a wide spot in Cat Point Creek, which flows into the Rappahannock River on its left side.

Manakin (PB 4:208) (1657)
Manoikin (PB 6:175) (1668)
Monocon (Richmond County Deed Book 3 [1697-1704]:96-99) (1685)
Monohan (Richmond County Deed Book 2:1693-1695]:228-229) (1697)

Place: Richmond County; near Cat Point Creek.

Monocon (Richmond County Deed Book 1 [1692-1693]:1-5) (1692)

MESSONGO

Creek: Accomack (Northampton) County; a tributary of Pocomoke Sound; near the Saxis Island Waterfowl Management Area.

Mesango (PB 5:181) (1662)
Massango (PB 6:314) (1670)
Mesangoe (PB 6:314) (1670)
Menssongo (PB 6:497) (1673)
Messongo (PB 6:529) (1674)

Masongo (Accomack County Deed, Wills, &c 1673-1676: 246) (1674)
Mosango (PB 6:638) (1678)
Masongo (Northampton County Orders, Wills 1674-1679:336) (1678)
Masongoes Branch (Northampton County Orders, Wills, Etc. 1698-1710:133) (1701)
Masongue (Northampton County Wills, Deeds, etc. 1718-1725:81) (1720)
Masongoe (Northampton County Wills and Inventories 1766-1772:238) (1769)

METOMKIN

Bay: Accomack County; behind Metompkin Island; on the seaside.

Metomkin (Boye map) (1826)

Branch: Accomack County; a branch of Metomkin Creek.

Mathomkin (PB 5:185) (1664)

Creeks (Great and Little): Accomack County; tributaries of Metomkin Bay, which is adjacent to Baylys Neck and the Atlantic Ocean. Parker Creek, on the north side of Baylys Neck, was known as Great Metomkin Creek; Walston Creek, on the south side of Baylys Neck, was known as Little Metomkin Creek

Matomkin (PB 4:287) (1659)
Matomkins (PB 5:184) (1663)
Matampken (Herrman map) (1670)
Matompkin (PB 6:396) (1672)
Mattomkin (PB 6:683) (1679)

Indian Town: Accomack County; sometimes called "Little Matomkin;" on Baylys Neck, on the left bank of Walston (formerly Little Metomkin) Creek.

Powhatan Indian Place Names in Tidewater Virginia

Pomunkin (FOR III:10:47) (1649)
Motomkin (Northampton County, Deeds and Wills 5:18) (1654)
Matompkin (PB 6:393) (1672)
Motompkin (PB 6:638) (1678)
Mattomkin (PB 7:647) (1688)
Matomkins (Accomack County, Wills and Orders 1682-1697:198) (1690)
Matomkin (Bruce, "Public Officers in Virginia, 1702, 1714, 363) (1702)

Inlet: Accomack County; between Cedar Island's Cedar Point, an unnamed island, and the Atlantic Ocean.

Metomkin (Boye map) (1826)

Island: Accomack County; southwest of Assawoman Island, between Metompkin Bay and the Atlantic Ocean.

Metomkin (Marzone map) (1855)

Place: Accomack County; possibly Matompkin Island.

Mattomkin (Northampton County Orders, Wills 1674-1679:336) (1678)
Matomkin (Northampton County Orders, Wills, Etc. 1689-1698:1) (1689)

Point: King George County; on the Potomac River's right bank; adjacent to Jones Pond and upstream from Chotank Creek; almost opposite the mouth of Nanjemoy Creek on the Maryland side.

Matomkin (Fry-Jefferson map) (1751)

MITCHAMOXEN

Place: Caroline County; on the Rappahannock River's right bank; on the south shore of Portobago Bay, west of Portobago Creek.

Mitchamoxen (Jefferson-Brooke map) (1747)

MOBJACK

Bay: Gloucester and Mathews Counties; tributary of the Chesapeake Bay north of the York River's mouth. It is uncertain whether Mobjack is an Indian name.

Mockjack (PB 1:759) (1640)
Mobjack (PB 1:804) (1642)
Mopjack (York County, Deeds, Wills and Orders 1:293) (1654)
Mockiack (PB 4:276) (1659)
Mockjeck (PB 7:518) (1686)

Path: Gloucester County; probably ran in a northeasterly direction from the head of Poropotank Creek; no known association with Mobjack Bay.
Mobjack (PB 3:7) (1654)

MOCKORN

Creek: Northampton County; probably modern Mockhorn Channel, part of the Intracoastal Waterway.

Mockhorn (Marzone map) (1855)

Island: Northampton County; on the seaside, between Mockhorn and Magothy Bays and the Atlantic Ocean; part of the barrier islands that Captain John Smith called "Smyths Iles."

Mockon (PB 4:87) (1657)
Mackone (PB 7:324) (1683)
Mokkon or Custis (Herrman map) (1670)
Mocken (Fry-Jefferson map) (1751)
Mockhorn (Boye map) (1826)

Powhatan Indian Place Names in Tidewater Virginia

MOKETE

Indian Town: Isle of Wight County; on the James River's right side, east of the Pagan River's mouth, near Rescue.

Mokete (Smith map) (1612)

MOMTAPWEAKE

Place: New Kent County; on the Chickahominy River's left bank, west of Lanexa.

Momtapweake (PB 1:643) (1639)

MONACK

Neck: City of Poquoson; on the left bank of the Northwest Branch of the Back River; where Brick Kiln Creek begins.

Monack (PB 1:317) (1635)
Moanack (PB 1:515) (1637)

Swamp: King and Queen County; near Dragon Swamp.

Monack (PB 10:15) (1711)

MONAHASSANUGH

Indian Town: Buckingham County; on the James River's right bank, above Wingina. Probably a Siouan-speaking Monacan name rather than an Algonquian-speaking Powhatan one.

Monahassanugh (Smith map) (1612)

MONASUKAPANOUGH

Indian Town: Goochland County; on the James River's left bank, above the fall line. Probably a Siouan-speaking Monacan name rather than an Algonquian-speaking Powhatan one.

Monasukapanough (Smith map) (1612)

MONCUSANECK

Creek or Run: Dinwiddie (formerly Prince George) County; a tributary on the Appomattox River's right side; near Cattail Branch of Rohoic (formerly Old Town and Indian Town) Creek; southwest of the City of Petersburg.

Moncus-a-neak (PB 7:707) (1689)
Moncasaneak (PB 8:74) (1690)
Moncuseneck (PB 8:244) (1692)
Monosoneck (PB 9:714) (1706)
Moccosonich (PB 10:52) (1711)
Monosinech (PB 10:335) (1717)
Moccosoneck (PB 10:337) (1717)
Monksneck (Wood map) (1820a)

Place: Prince George County; adjacent to Moncusaneck Creek.

Moncusenecke (PB 7:120) (1682)
Moncusoneck (PB 8:71) (1684)
Moncus-a-neck (PB 7:707) (1689)
Moncuseneck (PB 8:71) (1690)
Moncosaneak (PB 8:74) (1690)
Moncuse Neck (PB 8:149) (1691)
Moncusaneck (PB 8:315) (1694)
Moneasanock (PB 8:315) (1694)

Road: Prince George County; south of the Appomattox River's right bank; led to the Appomattox ferry.

Monkassaneck (Bristol Parish Vestry Book 24) (1727)
Monksneck (Wood map) (1820)

Powhatan Indian Place Names in Tidewater Virginia

Swamp: Dinwiddie (formerly Prince George, a descendant of Charles City) County; on the Appomattox River's right side; probably associated with Moncusaneck Creek; a few miles southwest of Petersburg.

Moncusenecke (PB 7:120) (1682)
Moncuseneck (PB 8:71) (1690)
Moncuse Neck (PB 8:149) (1691)
Muncusneck (PB 9:156) (1698)

MONDUI

Creek: Northampton County; a tributary of Nassawadox Creek.

Mondui (PB 1977: 97) (1671).

MORATTICO

Creek or River: Richmond County; a tributary on the Rappahannock River's left side and now known as Lancaster Creek; the name "Morattico" has shifted to a tributary on that creek's right side.

Macaughtions (MEADE II:478) (1651)
Moratcon (PB 3:129) (1652)
Morroticon (PB 3:172) (1652)
Morratico (PB 3:195) (1652)
Moraticon (PB 3:74) (1653)
Moraticond (PB 3:331) (1654)
Moratocond (PB 3:362) (1655)
Morraticon (PB 4:73) (1655)
Morratticon (PB 3:380) (1656)
Marattaco (Old Rappahannock County Deeds 2:39) (1658)
Moratticoe (PB 4:144) (1658)
Morratticoe (PB 4:252) (1658)
Morrattaquond (PB 4:472) (1660)
Moraticon (Old Rappahannock County Deed Book 1656-1664:233-234) (1663)
Morrattico (PB 4:125) (1664)
Narratico (PB 5:198) (1664)
Marattico (Old Rappahannock County Deeds 3: 356) (1667)
Marratecoe (PB 6:305) (1667)
Morattecoe (PB 6:318) (1670)
Marrattico (PB 6:654) (1678)
Morratter (Old Rappahannock County Deeds and Wills 1677-1682:247-251) (1679)
Morattico (Jefferson-Brooke map) (1747)
Moratico (Anonymous map) (1776)

Indian Town: Richmond County; on Lancaster (formerly Morratico) Creek's right bank; near Simonson. The chief of this tribe in 1651 may have been named Machamap (PP 118).

Marraughtacum (CJS I:53) (1608)
Moraughtacut (Zuniga map) (1608)
Moraughtacund (Smith map) (1612)
Moratoerin (MEADE II: 479) (1651)
Moraticond (PB 3:167) (1652)
Morraticon (PB 4:73) (1655)
Moratticoe (PB 4:240) (1658)
Moratticon (PB 5:339) (1662)
Maratico (Old Rappahannock County, Deeds 3:356) (1667)
Moratticum (Old Rappahannock County, Deeds 4:371) (1671)
Moratiquond (Old Rappahannock County, Deeds 4:529) (1672)

Path: Lancaster County; a trail leading from the Morratico Indian Town on Lancaster Creek to the Wiccocomico Indian Town on Indian Creek, a tributary of Fleet's Bay.

Moratico (PB 2:335) (1651)
Moraticon (PB 3:45) (1653)
Morattico (PB 4:113) (1657)
Morakio (Lancaster County Deeds and Wills 1661-1672:236) (1662)

Powhatan Indian Place Names in Tidewater Virginia

Point: Lancaster County; on the Rappahannock River's left bank, on the east side of the mouth of Lancaster Creek; now called Curletts Point, although "Morattico" is the name of the modern neighborhood.

Morratico (Jefferson-Brooke map) (1747)

MORINOGH

Indian Town: New Kent County; on the Chickahominy River's right bank; opposite Parsons Island and just below Diascund Creek's mouth.

Morinogh (CJS I:41) (1608)

MOROTSNY

Branch or Creek: Westmoreland County; a tributary on the Potomac River's right side; in the vicinity of Popes (Hallowes) Creek

Morakswee (PB 5:236) (1662)
Morotsny (PB 5:438) (1662)
Moscceway (Essex County Deeds and Wills 1692-1695:230) (1690)

MOUNTSACK

Place: Isle of Wight or Nansemond County; an Indian field on the Blackwater River "or toward the head of Chawon or Chawonock River;" possibly in North Carolina.

Mountsack (PB 6:45) (1667)

MOYAONS

Indian Town: in Maryland on the Potomac River's left bank, with the major town being on Piscataway Creek; the "town" seems to have extended across the Potomac into Fairfax County, Virginia – a not uncommon way that Algonquian-speakers thought about their territories. The community's inhabitants were later known as Piscataways, and still later as Conoys.

Moyaoncer (CJS I:55) (1608)
Moyaens (Velasco map) (1610)
Moyaones (CJS II:227) (1612)
Moyaons (VCR III:73) (1617

MOYSONEC

Indian Town: New Kent County; on the Chickahominy River's left bank; just upstream from Diascund Creek's mouth; near Nantepoy Run and Neck; the site of an English garrison erected in 1644-1645 to control the Indians' access to the James-York Peninsula.

Mosonok (Zuniga map) (1608)
Moysonec (Smith map) (1612)
Moysenac (Ogilby map) (1676)

MUSCONTE

Branch: Charles City County; a tributary on the Chickahominy River's right side; near Mattahunk Neck.

Musconte (PB 4:257) (1658)

MUSKETANK

Indian Town: various Southside Virginia counties possible; on the Nottoway or Meherrin Rivers; occupied by the Weyanock Indians during the early 1670s (Stanard, "Indians of Southern Virginia," 1).

Powhatan Indian Place Names in Tidewater Virginia

MUTTAMUSSENSACK

Indian Town: King and Queen County; on the Mattaponi River's left bank, near Rickahock.

Muttamussensack (Smith map) (1612)
Muttamussinsack (Velasco map) (1610)

MUTTNATE

Run: Charles City County; a tributary of the Chickahominy River from the right side near Mattahunk Neck; also may have beem known as Wickwas or Nickwas Run, which was in the same vicinity.

Muttnate (PB 2:329) (1651)
Muttuate (PB 2:329) (1651)

MUZAZIN

Swamp: Caroline County; a tributary on the Rappahannock River's right; near Peumansend Creek; opposite Nansemond Neck.

Uzougin (Old Rappahannock County Deeds 2:57) (1657)
Muzazin (PB 5:413) (1665)
Nanzenin (PB 5:533) (1666)
Manzinzin (PB 7:181) (1682)
Unzingin (Old Rappahannock County Order Book 1687-1692:232) (1691)
Uzenzen (PB 8:221) (1692)

MYGHTUCKPASSUN

Indian Town: King William County; on the Mattaponi River's right bank; across from the mouth of London Swamp and west of White Bank.

Myghtuckpassu (Smith map) (1612)

MYOMPS

Place: Fairfax or Prince William County; in the vicinity of Myomps or Dogue Island

Moyompo (VCR III:20) (1609)
Myomps (VCR III:20) (1609)

NAMASSINGAKENT

Indian Town: Fairfax County; between Accotink and Pohick Creeks.

Namassingakent (Smith map) (1612)

NAMEROUGHQUENA

Indian Town: Fairfax County; on the right side of the Potomac River above Little Hunting Creek; across from the town of Nacotchtank.

Nameroughquena (Smith map) (1612)

NAMOZINE

Creek: boundary between Dinwiddie, Amelia and Nottoway Counties; a tributary of the Appomattox River's right side. The name may not be Algonquian.

Namusend Creek (PB 10:336) (1717)
Nummisseen Creek (PB 11:43) (1720
Namosend (Bristol Parish Vestry Book, 6 (1721)
Numanseen (Bristol Parish Vestry Book, 23) (1725)
Namisseen (Bristol Parish Vestry Book, 25) (1725)

Powhatan Indian Place Names in Tidewater Virginia

Nemurseens (Bristol Parish Vestry Book, 35) (1727)
Nemurseens (Bristol Parish Vestry Book, 35) (1727)
Nemussens (Bristol Parish Vestry Book, 55) (1731)
Nummisseen (Bristol Parish Vestry Book, 66) (1732)
Namezeen (Fry-Jefferson map) (1751)
Namazeen (Fry-Jefferson map) (1751)
Namazen (Captaine map) (1781)

Ferry: Dinwiddie County; located on the northerly part of Namozine Creek, where the Namozine River Road crosses the creek and enters Amelia County.

Nemurssens (Bristol Parish Vestry Book, 37) (1727)

Road: Dinwiddie and Amelia Counties.

Namozine River (USGS Amelia quadrangle) (1894)

NANDTANGHTACUND

Indian Town: Caroline County; between Portobago Bay and Green (Meaders) Bay on the right side of the Rappahannock River; a king's house; village to which a colonist reportedly fled in 1613.

Nantaughtacun (Zuniga map) (1608)
Nantaugstacum (CJS I:53) (1608)
Nandtanghtacund (Smith map) (1612)
Nantaughtacund (CJS II:147) (1612)
Nonsowhaticond (HAILE 844) (1613)
Nandtaughtacund (CJS III:174) (1624)
Nantautacund (CJS III:177) (1624)

NANDUA

Creek: Accomack County; a tributary of the Chesapeake Bay; the name was originally applied to present Craddock (formerly Currituck) Creek.

Nundue (PB 2:178) (1649)
Nondui (PB 3:127) (1652)
Nondin (PB 3:127) (1652)
Nondewee (PB 4:501) (1652)
Nandewe (PB 4:205) (1658)
Nondices (PB 4:537) (1661)
Nonduy (PB 4:459) (1661)
Nantue (Herrman map) (1670)
Nanduee (Northampton County Orders 1664-1674:210) (1673)
Nandowe (Northampton County Deeds, Wills, Etc. 1680-1692:42) (1679)
Nandewe (PB 9:446) (1702)
Nanticoake (Northampton County Wills and Inventories, 1708-1717:59) (1709)
Andua (Northampton County Wills, Deeds, etc. 1711-1718:40) (1712)
Anndue (Northampton County Wills, Deeds, etc. 1711-1718:82) (1713)
Nandew (PB 10:332) (1717)
Nanduey (Northampton County Wills, Deeds, etc. 1711-1718:152) (1718)
Nandue (Northampton County Wills, Deeds, etc. 1718-1725:143) (1721)
Anduay (Northampton County Wills, Deeds, etc. 1718-1725:171) (1723)
Nandewey (Northampton County Wills and Inventories. 1733-1740:332) (1739)
Nantue (Fry-Jefferson map) (1751)
Nantuck (Henry map) (1770)
Nandua (Marzone map) (1855)

Indian Town: Accomack County; located somewhere on Nandua Creek.

Nandue (Northampton County, Deeds, Wills and Orders 3:135) (1648)
Nanduye (BEV 184) (1704)

Powhatan Indian Place Names in Tidewater Virginia

NANSEMOND

Bay: City of Suffolk, formerly Nansemond County; at the mouth of the Nansemond River.

Nanzemund (PB 1:222) (1635)

County: now City of Suffolk.

Nansimund (PB 2:151) (1644)
Nansimum (PB 2:85) (1647)
Nansemund (PB 2:125) (1647)
Nansimond (PB 2:60) (1648)
Nancemund (PB 2:148) (1648)
Nancimum (PB 2:204) (1649)
Nansemond (PB 2:258) (1650)
Nanzemond (PB 3:6) (1653)
Nanzamond (PB 3:17) (1653)
Nanzemum (PB 3:304) (1654)
Nancemond (PB 3:385) (1656)
Nansamond (PB 4:135) (1657)
Nansimum (Northampton County Orders 1657-1664:203) (1659)
Nancimond (PB 4:298) (1662)
Nancimund (PB 5:195) (1664)
Nanzemon (PB 6:310) (1670)
Nanzimond (PB 6:311) (1670)

Creek: City of Suffolk, formerly Nansemond County.

Nansemond (Fry-Jefferson map) (1751)

Indian Town: City of Suffolk, formerly Nansemond County; at the Nansemond River's junction with its Western Branch, apparently on all three points at that junction; near Reid's Ferry; a king's house. In ca. 1610, the main town was ruled by Weyhohomo, with Annapetough, Weywingopp, and Tirchtough ruling satellite towns (HAILE 625).

Nattamonge (Tyndall map) (1608)
Nandsamund (Velasco map) (1610)
Nandsamund (Smith map) (1612)
Nansemunde (HAILE 501) (1612)
Nansamund (CJS II:242) (1612)
Nansemum (HEN 1:315) (1646)

Indian Town: King George County; on the left side of the Rappahannock River, just downriver from Port Conway. In 1677, a chief named Pattanochus signed the Treaty of Middle Plantation on his people's behalf (PP 120).

Nanzemond (PB 3:310) (1654)
Nanzemum (PB 3:275) (1654)
Nanzemoon (Lancaster County Deeds and Wills 1652-1657:324) (1655)
Nancemum (PB 4:68) (1656)
Nanzimum (PB 4:89) (1657)
Nancimond (PB 4:98) (1657)
Nansemond (PB 4:132) (1657)
Nanzemond (Lancaster County Deeds and Wills 1654-1661:169) (1657)
Nanzemon (PB 4:123) (1664)
Nanzemun (PB 5:373) 1664)
Nanzemand (Old Rappahannock County, Deeds [1663-1668]:228) (1667)
Nanzemone (PB 6:88) (1667)
Nanzem (Old Rappahannock County Deeds, Wills, Inventories &c 1668-1672:228) (1670)
Nanzemund (HEN II:318) (1674)
Nanzimund (Old Rappahannock County, Deeds, Wills, Inventories &c 1682-1688:31) (1683)
Nansimond (PB 8:419) (1695)

Neck: King George County; on the left side of the Rappahannock River near Port Conway; site of the Nanzemond Indian Town. This native group has no known connection with the Nansemond Indians living on the right side of the James River, on the Nansemond River.

Powhatan Indian Place Names in Tidewater Virginia

Nanzemum (PB 3:280) (1654)
Nanzemund (Old Rappahannock County Order Book 1687-1692:232) (1691)

River: City of Suffolk, formerly Nansemond County; a tributary of the James River on its right side.

Nawsamond (CJS I:79n.) (1608)
Nansamunge (HEN I:141) (1629)
Nanzemund (PB 1:126) (1633)
Nansamund (PB 1:170) (1635)
Nanzamund (PB 1:396) (1638)
Nansamond (PB 2:368) (1641)
Nansemund (PB 1:917) (1643)
Nansimond (PB 4:2) (1644)
Nansemum (PB 2:82) (1646)
Nansemund (PB 2:125) (1647)
Nancemund (PB 2:148) (1648)
Nancimum (PB 2:204) (1649)
Nansemond (PB 2:258) (1650)
Nanzamond (PB 3:18) (1652)
Nansemum (PB 3:125) (1652)
Nanzemond (PB 3:19) (1653)
Nanzemun (PB 3:89) (1653)
Nanzemum (PB 3:304) (1654)
Nancemun (Northumberland County Wills, Inventories &c. 1652-1658:133) (1654)
Nancemum (PB 4:469) (1661)
Nancimond (PB 4:284) (1662)
Nancemun (PB 5:336) (1662)
Nancimun (PB 5:319) (1664)
Nanzmon (PB 6:310) (1670)
Nansemond (Anonymous map) (1776)

NANAPOYAC

Indian Town: Surry County; on the right side of the James River near Eastover; across from the mouth of the Chickahominy River.

Mantapoyok (Zuniga map) (1608)
Nantapoyac (Smith map) (1612)

Nanapoyack (Ogilby map) (1676)

NANTECOCK

Creek: New Kent County; probably a tributary of the Pamunkey River on its right side.

Nantecock (PB 9:664) (1705)

Neck: New Kent County; adjacent to the creek of the same name, which is located on the right side of the Pamunkey River.

Nantecock (PB 9:664) (1705)

NANTUPCOY

Neck: New Kent County; on the left side of the Chickahominy River; now a nameless neck of land adjacent to the upstream side of Diascund Creek's mouth.

Nantupcoy (PB 4:55) (1656)
Nantepoy (PB 7:96) (1681)

Run: New Kent County; on the left side of the Chickahominy River, adjacent to Diascund Creek and the neck of land formerly known as Nantepoy Neck.

Nantepoy (PB 7:96) (1681)

NANTYPOYSON

Creek: Lancaster County; a tributary of Little Bay, which in turn is a tributary of Fleet's Bay; now known as Antipoison Creek.

Nantipolzey (PB 4:140) (1657)
Nanty Poyson (PB 4:130) (1662)
Nanbypoyson (PB 4:308) (1662)

Powhatan Indian Place Names in Tidewater Virginia

Mantipoyson (Lancaster County Order Book 1656-1666:259) (1663)
Nantypoyson (PB 5:143) (1664)
Nantipoyson (PB 6:280) (1669)

Neck: Lancaster County; a neck overlooking Nantypoyson Creek.

Manipouson (Lancaster County Order Book 1656-1666:260) (1663)

Path: Lancaster County; in the vicinity of Antipoison Creek.

Nantopoizon (Lancaster County Deeds and Wills 1661-1672:399-400) (1700)

Point: Lancaster County; in the vicinity of Antipoison Creek.

Antepoison (Bache map) (1850)

NANZAMOXEN

Creek: King George County; on the left side of the Rappahannock River; now known as Millbank Creek.
Nanzamoxen (Jefferson-Brook map) (1747)

NANZATICO

Bay: King George County; on the left side of the Rappahannock River, across from Portobago Bay.

Nazattco (Anonymous map) (1776)
Nansatico (Bache map) (1854)

Indian Town: near the falls of the Potomac River, probably on the Maryland side.

Nazatica (CJS III: 312) (1624)

Indian Town: King George County; on the left side of the Rappahannock River, near Nanzatico Bay. In 1662 Attamahune was this tribe's chief; Pattanochus, a chief, signed the Treaty of Middle Plantation on their behalf in 1677 (PP 120).

Asasaticon (PB 4:10) (1655)
Nansatiquon (PB 4:51) (1656)
Nansatiquond (PB 4:98) (1657)
Nansatticoe (PB 4:245) (1657)
Nanzaticun (PB 5:236) (1662)
Noncottecoe (MCGC 493) 1662)
Ausaticon (PB 5:194) (1664)
Nanzatticon (PB 5:241) (1664)
Nansatequond (PB 5:384) (1664)
Nansatiquon (Old Rappahannock County Deeds and Wills 1656-1664:327) (1664)
Nansatigmond (Old Rappahannock County Deeds, Wills, Inventories 1665-1677:54) (1664)
Nansatiquand (Old Rappahannock County Deeds, Wills, Inventories 1672-1676:229) (1664)
Mansattero (Stafford County, Court Records 1664-68, 1689-93:10) (1664)
Nanzaticon (PB 5:413) (1665)
Monzation (MCGC 488) (1666)
Nanzatico (PB 6:62) (1667)
Nanzcattico (HEN II:275) (1669)
Nanjattico (Herrman map) (1670)
Nansatticcoe (PB 6:688) (1679)
Nanzattico (PB 7:34) (1680)
Nansiatico (EJC I:559) (1681)
Nanscatuo (SAIN 20:690) (1702)
Nanziaitico (HEN III:469) (1705)
Nansattico (Essex County, Orders 3:245) (1706)
Nanzattica (Fry-Jefferson map) (1751)

Path: King George and Westmoreland Counties; running on an east-west axis across the Northern Neck, from Nanzattico on the Rappahannock River

Powhatan Indian Place Names in Tidewater Virginia

to the right side of the Potomac and Nominy Creek.

Vasatican (PB 3:35) (1653)
Nungeocicoe (PB 3:276) (1654)
Nangatico (PB 4:313) (1661)
Nansaticoe (Westmoreland County, Deeds and Wills 1: 317) (1664)
Naniatico (PB 5:275) (1664)
Nanjattico (PB 7:47) (1680)

NASSAWADOX

Creek or River: Northampton County; a tributary of the Chesapeake Bay.

Nuswattocks (PB 1:539) (1638)
Nuswatocks (PB 1:698) (1640)
Nusswattockes (Northampton County Orders, Deeds, Wills &c 1640-1645:2) (1640)
Naswattocks (PB 1:854) (1642)
Nuswattock (Northampton County Orders, Deeds, Wills &c 1640-1645:217) (1642)
Nuswattcoke (Northampton County Orders, Deeds, Wills &c 1640-1645:232) (1642)
Nustsawattocke (PB 2:67) (1646)
Naswattock (PB 2:69) (1646)
Nasawattockes (PB 2:75) (1646)
Naswattocke (PB 2:75) (1646)
Noswattock (PB 2:184) (1649)
Nuswattucks (PB 3:311) (1654)
Nuswattocks (Northampton County Deeds, Wills, Etc. 1654-1655:56) (1654)
Nusswattox (Northampton County Deeds, Wills, Etc. 1657-1666:76) (1660)
Nuswattoke (PB 4:539) (1662)
Nunswattox (PB 5:388) (1665)
Nuswadox (PB 6:37) (1666)
Muswadox (PB 6:261) (1669)
Naswattics (Herrman map) (1670)
Nuswattox (PB 6:372) (1671)
Nasswattux (PB 6:608) (1676)
Nusswattux (PB 6:681) (1679)
Nusswaddox (Northampton County Orders, Wills, Etc. 1679-1683:249) (1680)
Nuswaddox (Northampton County Orders, Wills 1698-1710:68) (1700)
Nauswaudux (Northampton County Orders, Wills 1698-1710:163) (1703)
Nuswattox (PB 9:729) (1706)
Nurswatox (Northampton County Wills, Deeds, etc. 1711-1718:28) (1711)
Nusswaddux (Northampton County Wills, Deeds, etc. 1711-1718:105) (1713)
Neswaddux (PB 13:319) (1728)
Nuswattux (Northampton County Wills and Inventories, 1740-1750:23) (1737)
Nasswadox (Northampton County Wills and Inventories, 1740-1750:146) (1744)
Naswadox (Northampton County Wills and Inventories, 1740-1750:409) (1748)
Naswattix (Fry-Jefferson map) (1751)
Nasawadox (Marzone map) (1855)
Nassawadox (USDA Northampton County Sheet) (1917)

Indian Town: Northampton County; on the north side of Nassawadox Creek.

Naswattock (PB 2:227) (1650)
Nusattock (Northampton County Deeds, Wills &c 1654-1655:125) (1651)
Nuswittocks (Northampton County Deeds, Wills, &c 1654-1655:130) (1651)
Nuswattocks (PB 4:58) (1656)

Neck: Northampton County; on north side of Nassawadox Creek.

Nasswadox (Northampton County Wills and Inventories 1760-1762:123) (1760)
Naswaddax (Northampton County Wills and Inventories, 1772-1777:387) (1774)
Naswadux (Northampton County Wills and Inventories, 1772-1777:387) (1774)

Powhatan Indian Place Names in Tidewater Virginia

Nasswaddox (Northampton County Wills and Inventories, 1777-1783:574) (1774)

Place: Northampton County; in the vicinity of Nassawadox Creek.

Nuswattocks (Northampton County Orders, Deeds, Wills, Etc. 1640-1645:144) (1643)
Nasswatux (Northampton County Deeds, Wills, Etc. 1657-1666:27) (1658)
Nasswattokes (Northampton County Deeds, Wills, Etc. 1657-1666:64) (1659)
Nusswattux (Northampton County Deeds, Wills, Etc. 1657-1666:114) (1661)
Nuswattux (Northampton County Deeds, Wills, Etc. 1657-1666:140) (1662)
Nuswattox (Northampton County Orders 1679-1683:59) (1678)
Nurswattox (Northampton County Orders, Wills 1683-1689:400) (1688)
Nuswaddox (Northampton County Orders, Wills 1683-1689:367) (1688)
Nurswaddox (Northampton County Orders, Wills 1698-1710:68) (1700)
Nasswaddox (Northampton County Wills and Inventories, 1750-1754:325) (1751)

NAWACATEN

Indian Town: Westmoreland County; on the left side of the Rappahannock River; above the mouth of Peedee Creek.

Nawacaten (Smith map) (1612)

NAWNAUTOUGH

Indian Town: Richmond County; left side of the Rappahannock River; north of Little Carter Creek's mouth.

Nawnautough (Smith map) (1612)

NEABSCO

Creek: Prince William County; on the right side of the Potomac River; adjacent to Featherstone National Wildlife Refuge.

Niopsco (PB 4:143) (1657)
Nyopscoe (PB 4:195) (1658)
Niobscoe (PB 6:691) (1679)
Nyobscoe (PB 6:691) (1679)
Neapsco (Jefferson-Brooke map) (1747)

Place: Fairfax and/or Prince William Counties; somewhere near Occoquan.

Nieapside (Lancaster County Order Book 1666-1680:478) (1679)

NECHANICOK

Indian Town: Charles City County; on the right side of the Chickahominy River; on the downstream side of Stony Run's mouth.

Nachanicok (Zuniga map) (1608)
Nechanichock (CJS I:41) (1608)
Nechancicok (Smith map) (1612)

NECOTOWANCE

Creek: King William County; a tributary of the Pamunkey River on its left side; upstream from the Pamunkey Indian Reservation.

Nicatawance (PB 9:260) (1700)
Nickate Wance (PB 9:433) (1702)
Nicotiwance (PB 18:279) (1739)
Nicatiwan (Fry-Jefferson map) (1751)
Nickatewance (PB 33:621) (1759)
Nicatawan (Boye map) (1826)

Powhatan Indian Place Names in Tidewater Virginia

Path: Charles City County; on the left side of the Chickahominy River near Matahunk Neck.

Nicadawances (PB 3:389) (1656)
Nickadewans (PB 4:256) (1658)
Nickedewans (PB 7:124) (1682)
Nicketewances (PB 7:515) (1686)

Place: Charles City County; on the right side of Tomahund Creek's headwaters.

Nicatounces Quarter (PB 4:49) (1656)

Swamp: King William County; left side of the Pamunkey River; upstream from the Pamunkey Indian Reservation.

Nickaty Wance (PB 9:433) (1702)
Nicaty Wance (PB 9:435) (1702)
Nicatowance (Gilmer map) (1864b)

NEHUNTAS

Creek: Norfolk County, now the city of Chesapeake; on the south side of the eastern branch of the Elizabeth River, probably to the east of Indian Creek.

Nehuntas (PB 1:539) (1637)
Nelruntrees (PB 6:148) (1668)

NEPAWTACUM

Indian Town: Lancaster County; on the left side of the Rappahannock River on Orchard Point.

Nepawtacum (Smith map) (1612)

NESUMS

Creek: Lancaster County; in the vicinity of White House Creek and west of the Corotoman River's mouth.

Nesums (Jefferson-Brooke map) (1747)

NICKAHOOKE

Branch: New Kent County; a tributary of Totopotomoy Creek, which is a tributary of the Pamunkey River's right side.

Nickahooke (PB 7:42) (1680)

NICKAWAMPUS

Creek: Accomack County; a tributary of Wachapreague Channel and the Atlantic Ocean; its headwaters are near Melfa.

Nickowomsim (PB 6:396) (1672)
Nicowomson (Accomack County, Wills 1671-1673: 213) (1673)
Niccowomson (Accomack County, Wills 1673-1676:14) (1673)
Nickowansin (Accomack County, Wills 1673-1676: 135) (1674)
Niccowamson (Accomack County Wills and Orders 1682-1697:198) (1690)

NIMCOCK

Creek: Middlesex County; on the right side of the Rappahannock River; now known as Urbanna Creek.

Nimcock (PB 2:271) (1650)
Nymcock (PB 2:341) (1651)
Myem Cocke (PB 4:68) (1653)
Nyemcock (PB 3:69) (1653)
Niemcock (PB 4:27) (1656)
Newcock (Old Rappahannock County Deeds, Wills, Inventories &c 1656-1664:130) (1657)
Nanncock (Old Rappahannock County Deeds, Wills, Inventories &c 1656-1662:33) (1658)

Powhatan Indian Place Names in Tidewater Virginia

Naimcock (Old Rappahannock County Deeds, Wills, Inventories &c 1656-1662:33) (1658)
Mimcock (PB 6:51) (1661)
Nimcocke (PB 5:345) (1663)
Naemcock (PB 6:463) (1673)

Indian Towns (Old and New): Middlesex County; on the right side of the Rappahannock River; east of Rosegill Creek.

Nimcock (PB 2:170-171) (1649)

NOMINI

Bay: Westmoreland County; on the right side of the Potomac River; at Kingcopsico Point and Currioman Bay.

Nomeny (PB 2:206) (1649)
Nomony (Jefferson-Brooke map) (1747)
Nomini (Fry-Jefferson map) (1751)
Nominy (Henry map) (1770)

Creek and River: Westmoreland County; on the right side of the Potomac River; tributary of Nomini Bay.

Nomeny (PB 2:283) (1650)
Nomini (PB 2:337) (1651)
Nomany (PB 3:3) (1653)
Nominy (PB 4:50) (1656)
Nominie (PB 5:527) (1666)
Nominye (Herrman map) (1670)
Nonomy (Jefferson-Brooke map) (1747)

Ferry: Westmoreland County; on Nomini Creek at Mount Holly; now replaced by the Nomini Bridge on County Route 220.

Nomini (USGS Montross quadrangle) (1890)

Indian Town: Westmoreland County; on the west side of Nomini Creek; a king's house.

Onamione (Zuniga map) (1608)
Onawmament (Velasco map) (1610)
Nomini (Smith map) (1612)
Onawmanient (CJS II:148) (1612)
Nominy (PB 2:278) (1650)
Nomeny (PB 3:3) (1653)
Nomany (PB 4:121) (1662)

Parish: Westmoreland County; formed in 1653 from the northwestern portion of Northumberland County; became extinct around 1668 (DVA 166-167; HEN I:352; II:285).

Path: Westmoreland County; near Lower Machodoc Creek.

Nomany (PB 4:314) (1661)

OATSPAKETY

Creek: on the left side of the Rappahannock River; possibly the same as Totuskey Creek.

Oatspakety (PB 5:240) (1662)

OCCOCONSON

Place: Accomack County; somewhere near the head of Occohannock Creek.

Occocomson (PB 5:187) (1664)
Occaconson (Accomack County, Orders 1676-1678:80) (1677)
Occocomsan (Northampton County Orders, Wills 1674-1679:336) (1678)

Powhatan Indian Place Names in Tidewater Virginia

Ockocomson (Northampton County Deeds, Wills, Etc. 1680-1692:42) (1679)
Accocomson (PB 7:66) (1680)
Acaconson (Northampton County Wills, Deeds, etc. 1711-1718:58) (1708)

OCCOHANNOCK

Creek: part of the boundary between Accomack and Northampton Counties; a tributary of the Chesapeake Bay.

Acohanock (CJS II:150) (1612)
Aquohanock (CJS III:289) (1624)
Occahannocke (Northampton County Deeds, Wills, Etc. 1654-1655:102) (1645)
Otchahannock (PB 2:115) (1648)
Occohannocke (PB 2:159) (1648)
Occahanock (PB 2:177) (1649)
Occhanock (PB 2:177) (1649)
Occahannocke (PB 2:178) (1649)
Ockahannock (PB 2:221) (1650)
Accahannock (PB 2:272) (1650)
Occahanocke (Northampton County Deeds, Wills, Etc. 1651-1654:64) (1651)
Occahaincock (PB 2:314) (1651)
Accohanock (PB 2:324) (1651)
Ocahannock (PB 3:7) (1653)
Occohanock (PB 3:288) (1654)
Occahamack (PB 3:296) (1654)
Ockahanock (Northampton County Deeds, Wills, Etc. 1657-1666:7) (1657)
Ocahanocke (PB 4:140) (1658)
Ochanocke (PB 4:140) (1658)
Ockahanock (PB 4:455) (1660)
Occahannock (Northampton County Deeds, Wills, Etc. 1657-1666:76) (1660)
Occohanneck (PB 5:491) (1666)
Accahanock (Herrman map) (1670)
Ochahannocks (PB 6:608) (1676)
Occohannock (Northampton County Orders, Wills 1683-1689:24) (1683)
Occahannock (Northampton County Orders, Wills 1683-1689:124) (1684)
Ochohanock (Northampton County Orders, Wills 1689-1698:7) (1689)
Occohanock (Northampton County Orders, Wills 1698-1710:198) (1704)
Occohannock (Northampton County Wills, Deeds, etc. 1708-1717:4) (1708)
Ocohanock (Northampton County Wills, Deeds, etc. 1711-1718:113) (1713)
Oceahanork (Northampton County Deeds, Wills, Etc. 1725-1733:171) (1728)
Ockkahannock (Northampton County Wills and Inventories. 1733-1740:332) (1739)
Occahanock (Northampton County Wills and Inventories 140-1750:129) (1744)
Occahanack (Northampton County Wills, Etc. 1792-1795:120) (1791)

Indian Town: Northampton County; somewhere between the headwaters of Occohannock and Nassawadox Creeks; a king's house. In the 1620s, Kiptopeke, a younger brother of the Accomac chief who was based at this town, governed the northern half of the Virginia Eastern Shore on his brother's behalf; by 1643, his successor was Wackawamp (deceased by 1649); he was followed by Tapatiaton ("Debbedeavon"), who was dead by 1672 (PP 124, 125-26).

Accohanock (Smith map) (1612)
Occahannock (PB 4:466) (1661)
Accohanock (Ogilby map) (1676)
Occahamock (DES 66) (1699)

Parish: Northampton County; formed in 1652 and in 1663 when Northampton County was divided into two counties, it became part of Accomack Parish (DSVA 189-190).

Ocquhanocke (HEN I:374) (1652)

Powhatan Indian Place Names in Tidewater Virginia

Path: Northampton County; near the head of a branch of Nassawadox Creek.
Occahannocke (PB 4:63) (1655)
Ockahanock (PB 4:230) (1658)
Occahanoke (PB 6:600) (1676)

Place: Northampton County; somewhere on the ridge or neck of land between Occohannock and Nassawadox Creeks.

Acohannock (Northampton County Wills, Deeds &c. 1711-1718:53) (1713)
Accohanack (Northampton County Wills, Deeds &c. 1711-1718:105) (1713)

OCCOQUAN

Bay: Fairfax and Prince William Counties; at the mouth of the Occoquan River, on the right side of the Potomac River.

River: part of the boundary line between Fairfax and Prince William Counties; a tributary of the Potomac River's right side.

Aquoconde (PB 3:17) (1653)
Ohoquin (PB 5:285) (1654)
Aquaconde (PB 4:118) (1657)
Ochaquim (PB 4:143) (1657)
Ohaquinn (PB 4:192) (1657)
Aquacon (Northumberland County Wills, Inventories &c 1652-1658:143) (1658)
Accaquon (PB 5:526) (1666)
Oquaquon (PB 6:295) (1669)
Occkaquon (PB 6:289) (1670)
Achquin (Herrman map) (1670)
Occoquan (Jefferson-Brooke map) (1747)

OCCANEECHI

Path: Prince George County; on the north side of Bear Swamp, leading southward toward the island home of the Occaneechi Indians, a Siouan-speaking tribe. It is uncertain whether "Occaneechi" was those people's name for themselves, or the name the Algonquian-speaking Powhatans called them.

Occounche (PB 10:337) (1717)

Swamp: Prince George and Isle of Wight Counties.

Occanecee Swamp (PB 10:425) (1719)
Occaneecy Swamp (PB 11:56) (1720)

OCCUPACIA

Creek: Essex County; on the right side of the Rappahannock River; near Bottoms Neck.

Occapason (PB 3:142) (1652)
Occapacon (PB 4:77) (1659)
Occopason (PB 4:301) (1661)
Occapaton (PB 4:77) (1662)
Occupason (PB 5:353) (1662)
Occupare (PB 5:407) (1665)
Occupasion (PB 6:3) (1666)
Occupacon (PB 6:3) (1666)
Occupaice (Old Rappahannock County Deeds and Wills 1677-1682:201) (1666)
Occupaso (PB 6:194) (1668)
Ohcapce (PB 6:320) (1670)
Ocapaceo (PB 6:436) (1672)
Ocapesee (PB 6:436) (1672)
Occopace (PB 6:489) (1673)
Occapaceee (PB 6:532) (1674)
Occupation (PB 8:113) (1690)
Occapaccon (PB 8:144) (1690)
Occopace (Essex County Deeds and Wills 1692-1695:35-36) (1692)
Occupacon (Essex County Deeds and Wills 1692-1695:62-63) (1692)

Powhatan Indian Place Names in Tidewater Virginia

Occupatee (Essex County Deeds and Wills 1692-1695:387) (1692)
Occupatia (PB 8:360) (1694)
Occupacee (Essex County Deeds and Wills 1695-1699:332) (1699)
Occupacon Creek (PB 9:597) (1704)
Occupacy (Jefferson-Brooke map) (1747)
Occupacy (Fry-Jefferson map) (1751)
Occupacia (Gilmer map) (1864a)

OCHAHANNAUKE

Indian Town: King William or adjacent county; probably on the Pamunkey River; location uncertain. In ca. 1610, Uropaack was the chief in this town (HAILE 628).

Ochahannauke (HAILE 628) (1612).

OHOREEK

Swamp: part of the boundary between Surry and Prince George Counties; the headwaters of Upper Chippokes Creek on the James River's right side.

Ohoreek (PB 3:322) (1654)

OMOY

Creek: King George County; on the Rappahannock River's left side; now known as Millbank Creek.

Omoy (Herrman map) (1670)
Omen (Jefferson-Brooke map) (1747)

ONACHYMOYES

Place: Richmond County; three miles up Totuskey Creek, a tributary of the Rappahannock River's left side.

Onachymoyes Quarter (PB 4:282) (1654)

ONANCOCK

Creek: Accomack County; a tributary of the Chesapeake Bay.

Anancock (PB 3:339) (1655)
Oanancock (Northampton County Orders 1657-1664:8) (1657)
Anoncock (Accomack County Deeds and Wills 1663-1666:21) (1663)
Wanancook (Accomack County Deeds and Wills 1664-1671:168) (1670)
Onankok (Herrman map) (1670)
Anoncock Creek (PB 9:136) (1698)
Onancock (Marzone map) (1855)

Indian Town: Accomack County; somewhere near Onancock Creek. In the early 1660s, the chief was named Ekeeks (PP 126).

Occancocke (Northampton County Orders, Deeds, Wills &c 1651-1654:225) (1654)
Oanancocke (Northampton County Orders, Deeds, Wills &c 1651-1654:255) (1654)
Onankok (Herrman map) (1670)
Onancok (Accomack County, Deeds, Wills and Orders 1678-1682:13) (1678)
Oanancock (BEV 184) (1704)

Place: Accomack County; somewhere near Onancock Creek.

Owanancock (Northampton County Orders, Deeds, Wills &c 1640-1645:15) (1640)
Onancocke (Northampton County Orders, Deeds, Wills &c 1651-1654:144) (1652)

Powhatan Indian Place Names in Tidewater Virginia

OPAHOCK

Indian Town: Charles City County; on the Chickahominy River's right side; between Sunken Marsh and Mount Airy.

Opahock (Zuniga map) (1608)

OPPACTENOKE

Creek: King and Queen County; now called Garretts Creek, a tributary of the Mattaponi River's left side.

Oppactenoke (PB 4:467) (1660)

OPISCATUMECK

River: ancient Indian name for the Rappahannock River.

Opiscatumeck (HAILE 605) (1612)

OPISCOPANK

Creek: Middlesex County; a tributary of the Rappahannock River on its right side; possibly Lagrange Creek.

Episkapanke (PB 1:916) (1643)
Ekepaco (PB 6:296) (1670)
Ekepace Creek (PB 9:667) (1705)

Indian Town: Middlesex County; on the Rappahannock River's right side; between Lagrange and Urbanna Creeks; a king's house.

Opiscopank (Smith map) (1612)

OQUOMOCK

Indian Town: Richmond County; on the Rappahannock River's left side; on the upstream side of Farnham Creek's mouth.

Oquomock (Smith map) (1612)

OQUONOCK or OQUSNOCK

Indian Town: New Kent County; on the right side of the Pamunkey River's mouth; in the vicinity of Eltham Marsh and Mill Creek.

Oquonock or Oqusnock (Zuniga map) (1608)

ORACON

Creek: King and Queen County; just north of Exol Swamp, a tributary of Dragon Swamp.

Oracon (Gilmer map) (1864a)

ORAPAGUS

Creek: New Kent County; a tributary of the Pamunkey River's right side; now known as Big Creek.

Orapagus (Langston map) (1662)

ORAPAX

Indian Town: New Kent County; at the head of Black Creek, a tributary of the Pamunkey River's right side, in the Chickahominy River's headwaters; a king's house, occupied by Powhatan from 1609 to ca. 1613

Orohpikes (HAILE 483) (1610)
Oropikes (HAILE 486) (1610)
Orapaks (Smith map) (1612)
Orapakes (CJS II:147) (1612)
Orapacks (CJS II:173) (1612)

Powhatan Indian Place Names in Tidewater Virginia

ORAPEAK

Creek and Swamp: City of Suffolk (formerly Nansemond County); now known as Cypress Creek and Swamp. A community called Corapeake is located just south of the border between Virginia and North Carolina.

Orapeak (PB 7:196) (1682)
Coropeake (PB 9:277) (1700)
Orapeak (Fry-Jefferson map) (1751)

Place: City of Suffolk, formerly Nansemond County; in the Upper Parish; on the west side of the Great Dismal Swamp.

Orapeak (PB 7:196) (1682)

OROCCOCK

Branch: Prince George County; a tributary of Great Reedy Branch, which in turn is a tributary of Flowerdew Hundred Creek on the James River's right side; possibly Nobles Swamp.

Oroccock (PB 11:205) (1723)

OSAMKATECK

Indian Town: King William County; on the left side Pamunkey River; in the immediate vicinity of the Pamunkey Indian Reservation. Note: Captain John Smith's 1612 map puts Accosuwinck in this location.

Osamkateck (Zuniga map) (1608)

OTTACHUGH

Indian Town: Lancaster County; on the Rappahannock River's left side; between Cherry and Mosquito Points.

Ottachugh (Smith map) (1612)

OZAIAWOMEN

Indian Towns: King George County; on the Potomac River's right side; on both sides of Upper Machodoc Creek.

Ozaiawomen (Smith map) (1612)

OZENICK

Indian Town: James City County; on the Chickahominy River's left side; near Uncles Neck and Hog Neck Creek; later the site of the Wahrani Indian town.

Oraniocke (CJS I:41) (1608)
Ozanieck (Zuniga map) (1608)
Ozenick (Smith map) (1612)
Ozenies (CJS III: 303) (1624)
Ozinieke (CJS III: 316) (1624)
Ozinies (CJS III: 256) (1624)

PACOSOMACO

Creek: King William County; a tributary of the Pamunkey River on its left side; in the vicinity of Moncuin Creek.

Pacosomaco (PB 9:503) (1702)

PAEMOTINCK

Place: The Powhatan Indian name for the Appalachian Mountains.

Powhatan Indian Place Names in Tidewater Virginia

Paemotinck (LED 9) (1670)

PAMAMOMECK

Indian Town: King William County; below Jack's Creek, a tributary of the Pamunkey River's left side, and just upstream from the Pamunkey Indian Reservation.

Pamamomeck (Langston map) (1662)

PAMAREKE

Indian Town: King William County; on the Pamunkey River's left side; possibly same as the Pamunkey Indian Town. In ca. 1610, the chief in this town was Attasquintan (HAILE 628).

Pamareke (HAILE 628) (1612)

PAMPATIKE

Creek: King William County; on the Pamunkey River's left side; close to The Meadows and Moncuin Creek.

Pamptike (PB 7:13) (1679)
Pampertike (PB 7:121) (1682)
Pampatike (PB 9:594) (1704)
Ferry Landing and Place: King William County; on the Pamunkey River's left side; downstream from The Meadows.

Pamptike (PB 7:13) (1679)
Pampertike (PB 7:121) (1682)
Panatike (Gilmer map) (1864b)

PAMUNCOROY

Indian town: New Kent County; on Pamunkey River's right side; close to Rockahock Bar and upstream from White House Creek.

Pamakroy (Zuniga map, 1608)
Pamuncoroy (Smith map) (1612)

PAMUNN

Place: New Kent County; the rounded land form adjacent to Eltham Marsh.

Pamunn (Langston map) (1662)

PAMUNKEY

Indian Town: King William County; on the Pamunkey River's left side; between Cohoke and Herrick Creeks; a king's house. In the early 1600s, Opitchapam, Opechancanough, and Kekataugh, younger brothers of Powhatan, ruled this tribe; the longest-lived brother, Opechancanough, continued to govern until 1646, when he was succeeded by Necotowance. By the mid-1650s, Tottopottomoy was the chief; he was succeeded by Cockacoeske until her death in 1686 (PP 10 et passim, 87ff., 91ff., 98ff.)

Pamonke (Tyndall map) (1608)
Pamunkey (Smith map) (1612)
Pamunkie (BEV 184) (1704)

Indian Reservation: King William County; the peninsula between Cohoke and Old Town Creeks.

Neck: King William County; the land between the Pamunkey and Mattaponi Rivers.

Permunckey (PB 6:294) (1670)
Pommoncky (Essex County Deeds and Wills 1695-1699:316-317) (1698)

Powhatan Indian Place Names in Tidewater Virginia

Path: Charles City County; below the head of Chickahominy Swamp

Pamunkey (PB 5:367) (1664)
Pomonkey (PB 6:352) (1671)

Path: King William County; leading up Pamunkey Neck; beyond Cohoke Creek. Possibly an extension of the path of the same name in Charles City County.

Permunckey (PB 6:290) (1670)
Pamunkey (PB 6:294) (1670)

Place: King William County; on the Pamunkey River's left side; between Cohoke and Herrick Creeks; the territory of the Pamunkey Indians.

Pamonkie (HAILE 97) (1607)
Pamaunche (BAR I:93) (1607)
Pamaunke (BAR I:97) (1607)
Pamaunck (CJS I:47) (1608)
Pamauncke (CJS I:53) (1608)
Pamunke (CJS I:81) (1608)
Pamunka (CJS I:91) (1608)
Pamaonche (HAILE 195) (1608)
Pamaonke (HAILE 196) (1608)
Powmunkey (ARBER I:civ) (1610)
Pacomunky (VCR III:595) (1622)
Pawmunkie (VCR IV:9) (1623)
Pamaunkok (VCR IV:37) (1623)
Pomunkey (PB 2:62) (1646)
Pamunkey (PB 3:34) (1653)
Pomunke (PB 5:430) (1664)
Pamunckies (HEN II:275) (1669)
Pemaeoncock (LED 15) (1670)
Pammomock (Herrman map) (1670)
Pomunki (MCGC 370-371) (1674)
Pamamuch (SAIN 1:22) (1689)

River: the boundary between King William and New Kent Counties; unites with the Mattaponi River at West Point to form the York River; the name originally was applied solely to the York River.

Youghtanan (CJS I:51) (1608)
Pamaonche (HAILE 185) (1608)
Pamaunks (CJS I:63) (1608)
Pamaunk (Smith map) 1612
Pamunck (HAILE 603) (1612)
Pamunky (HAILE 652) (1612)
Pamaunkie (HAILE 843) (1614)
Pacomunky (VCR III:495) (1622)
Pamunckey (VCR IV:190) (1623)
Pamaunkee (CJS III:114) (1624)
Pamunkye (PB 1:369) (1630)
Pamunkey (PB 1:104) (1632)
Pamaunk (Vingboon map) (1639)
Pamunkie (PB 1:686) (1639)
Pomunckye (HEN I:287) (1644)
Pomunkey (PB 2:62) (1646)
Pamunkee (PB 2:309) (1650)
Pamonkey (PB 4:307) (1662)
Pamunk (Langston map) (1662)
Pomonkey (PB 6:191) (1668)
Pomonkey (Seib map) (1858)

PAPACOONE

Island: James City County; on the Chickahominy River's right side; within Diascund Creek; now known as Hicks Island.

Papacoone (PB 4:55) (1656)

PAPATACON

Creek: Essex County; somewhere near Beaverdam and Green Swamps.

Papatacon (Essex County Deeds and Wills 1695-1699:94-95) (1697)

PAPISCONE

Indian Town: King George County; on

Powhatan Indian Place Names in Tidewater Virginia

the Rappahannock River's left side; west of Gingoteague Creek.

Papiscone (Smith map) (1612)

PARACONOS

Indian town: Hanover County; on the Pamunkey River's right side; opposite Pampetike Landing. William Strachey identified this village as Baraconos; however, linguistically it is unlikely that the name began with a "B" (no other recorded Powhatan words did). In ca. 1610, the petty chief ruling this town was Attossamunek (HAILE 628).

Parokonosko (Zuniga map) (1608)
Paraconos (HAILE 628) (1612)

PARRAKETO

Point: City of Suffolk (formerly Nansemond County); on the Nansemond River's right side, above Bennetts Creek; now called Town Point; possibly not an Indian name.

Paraketo (PB 1:170) (1635)
Parraketo (PB 1:459) (1637)

PASATINCK

Creek: Caroline (formerly Essex) County; on the Rappahannock River's right side, downstream from Skinkers Neck; now called Mount Creek and Swamp.

Pasatinck (PB 3:280) (1654)
Passatink (PB 7:689) (1688)
Papetuck (Richmond County Orders 1694-1699:31) (1695)
Pasatank (Jefferson-Brooke map) (1747)

Run: Caroline (formerly Essex) County; on the Rappahannock River's right side; the headwaters of Pasatinck Creek.

Passating Run (PB 9:511) (1702)

PASAUGHTACOCK

Indian Town: King and Queen County; on the York River's left side and upstream from Hockley Creek.

Pasaughtacock (Smith map) (1612)

PASPAHEGH

Creek: Charles City County; tributary of the Chickahominy River's right side formerly Moyses, now Morris, Creek.

Tanks Pasbye Hayes (PB 1:362) (1636)
Tanks Pasbyhayes (PB 1:379) (1636)
Tanckes Pasbyhaies (PB 1:753) (1640)
Tancks Pasbehaies (PB 3:291) (1653)

Indian Towns and Territory: James City and Charles City Counties; on both sides of the Chickahominy River's mouth and extending upstream for several miles. Early English records did not distinguish between these Indians' towns and territory. A king's house was located in Charles City County just west of Sandy Point; the chief living there was named Wowinchopunck (PP 23 et passim).

Paspeians (CJS I:82) (1607)
Paspeiouh (HAILE 103) (1607)
Paspeiouk (HAILE 117) (1607)
Paspaheigh (BAR 214) (1608)
Paspeheagh (Tyndall map) (1608)
Paspaheighe (HAILE 192) (1608)
Paspihe (HAILE 92) (1608)
Paspihae (HAILE 94) (1608)

Powhatan Indian Place Names in Tidewater Virginia

Paspiha (HAILE 95) (1608)
Paspahegh (Smith map) (1612)
Paspihas (HAILE 138) (1612)
Paspaheans (HAILE 509) (1612)
Paspahe (HAILE 512) (1612)
Paspahae (HAILE 831) (1614)
Paspeheies (VCR III:99) (1618)
Paspaheigho (VCR III:255) (1620)
Paspehay (PB 1:1) (1621)
Passbehay (VCR III:623) (1622)
Paspaheg (CJS III:236) (1624)
Paspahege (CJS III:303) (1624)
Pasbeyheys (PB 1:137) (1632)
Pasbye Hayes (PB 1:397) (1636)
Old Pasbye Hayes (PB 1:469) (1637)
Pasbyehaies (PB 1:756) (1641)
Pasbyhaies (PB 1:756) (1641)

Place: New Kent County; near Cattail Swamp and a branch of Diascund Creek and Swamp.

Tancks Pasbehaies (PB 4:101) (1657)
Tankes Pasbehaies (PB 4:117) (1664)

PASPANEGH

Indian Town: Charles City County; on the Chickahominy River's right side; on Matahunk Neck.

Paspnegh (Zuniga map) (1608)
Paspaheigh (Velasco map) (1610)
Paspanegh (Smith map) (1612)

PASSAPATANZY

Creek and Run: King George County; on the Potomac River's right side between Belvedere and Fairview Beaches.

Pesbetansey (PB 3:132) (1652)
Paspetanzey (PB 4:219) (1658)
Pasbetancy (PB 5:233) (1662)
Pasbetank (PB 5:234) (1662)
Pasbitansy (PB 5:244) (1662)
Pasbytansee (PB 5:271) (1663)
Pasbetansey (PB 6:125) (1668)
Pasbetan (PB 6:257) (1669)
Pasbytanzey (Stafford County Record Book 1686-1693:20) (1685)
Pasbitanzie (Stafford County Record Book 1686-1693:113) (1688)
Paspitanzy (Stafford County Record Book 1686-1693:152) (1690)
Pasbetanzy (Stafford County Record Book 1686-1693:185) (1691)
Pasbetanzce (Richmond County Deed Book 2 [1693-1695]:75) (1694)
Paspatansy (Fry-Jefferson map) (1751)
Paspatansy (Anonymous map) (1776)
Paspatansa (Madison map) (1807)
Paspatansey (Tatham map) (1813)
Passapatanzy (USGS Fredericksburg quadrangle) (1888)

Indian Town: King George County; on the Potomac River's right side in the vicinity of Belvedere Beach. In 1610-1614, Iopassus (Japazaws) governed this small town as a viceroy for his brother, the paramount chief of Patawomeck (HAILE 658).

Pasptans (HAILE 489) (1610)
Pasptanse (HAILE 489) (1610)
Pastanzo (HAILE 606) (1612)
Pastancie (HAILE 753) (1613)
Pastancy (HAILE 754) (1613)
Passpatansey (Braden map) (185[-])

Place: King George County; on the Potomac River's right side.

Pasbetanzy Forest (Stafford County Record Book 1686-1693:172a) (1688)

PASSAUNKACK

Indian town: King William County; on

Powhatan Indian Place Names in Tidewater Virginia

the side of the Mattaponi River's right side, upstream from Aylett.

Passaunkack (Smith map) (1612)

PASTCOCK

Creek: King and Queen County; on the Mattaponi River's left side; east of the courthouse; now known as Mitchell Creek

Pastecock (Fry-Jefferson map) (1751)
Pastcock (Captaine map) (1781)

PAWCOCOMOCAC

Indian Town: Lancaster County; on the Rappahannock River's left side; west of Bertrand.

Pawcocomocac (Smith map) (1612)

PECKATOWNS

Place: Westmoreland County; north-northeast of the head of Lower Machodoc Creek.

Peckatowns (PB 5:393) (1664)

PEMACREY

Neck: New Kent County; on the Chickahominy River's right side; now known as Turners Neck.

Pemacrey (PB 4:55) (1656)

PEMINOE

Creek: Accomack County; northeast of Capeville; on the seaside.

Pemenoec (PB 1:615) (1638)

Pemino (PB 1:637) (1638)
Peminoe (PB 1:637) (1638)
Pemmonoe (Accomack County Court Records 1640-1645:9) (1640)
Penninoe (PB1:852) (1642)
Pemino (PB 6:608) (1676)

Place: Accomack County; in the upper part of the county; on the seaside.

Piminoe (PB 4:164) (1658)
Pemino (PB 6:608) (1676)
Pimeno (PB 6:608) (1676)

PEPETICO

Branch, Creek, and Swamp: King and Queen County; on the York River's left side; near the Mattaponi River's mouth; probably Goalders Creek.

Popetyke (PB 3:84) (1653)
Pepetico (PB 3:310) (1654)
Papatico (PB 5:278) (1663)
Papetico (PB 7:284) (1683)
Pepettico (PB 9:3) (1695)
Papetticoe (PB 9:96) (1697)
Tapstico (PB 9:122) (1697)
Pagetico (PB 9:558) (1703)
Pagetico (PB 9:588) (1702)
Pesticock (PB 9:655) (1705)
Pepetice (Fry-Jefferson map) (1751)
Peptice (Anonymous map) (1776)

PERPERTOCKS

Creek: King George County; on the Rappahannock River's left side; now known as Peedee Creek.

Popetick (PB 3:113) (1652)
Pepetick (PB 3:59) (1653)
Pepeticke (Old Rappahannock County Record Book 1656-1662:52) (1653)

Powhatan Indian Place Names in Tidewater Virginia

Peptick (Old Rappahannock County Record Book 1656-1662:84) (1653)
Pepoticke (PB 4:42) (1656)
Pepticke (Old Rappahannock County Deed Book 1656-1664:194) (1656)
Pepeticke (PB 4:89) (1662)
Papaticke (PB 4:278) (1662)
Perpetick (PB 6:122) (1668)
Papetuck (Richmond County Orders 1694-1699:31) (1695)
Papeta (Richmond County (Richmond County Deed Book 2 [1693-1695]:210-211) (1696)

PEUMANSEND

Creek, Run, and Swamp: Caroline County; on the Rappahannock River's right side; southerly branch of Mill Creek; downstream from Port Royal.

Puamunaremo (PB 5:138) (1663)
Puamunvein (PB 5:147) (1664)
Powmansend (PB 5:407) (1665)
Pwomansend (PB 6:28) (1667)
Pwomunzeene (PB 6:66) (1667)
Puamuslen (Herrman map) (1670)
Puemondsem (PB 6:286) (1670)
Puesmonseen (PB 6:286) (1670)
Pewamanesee (PB 6:490) (1673)
Pumans Inn: (Old Rappahannock County Wills 1682-1687:13-15) (1679)
Pewomansin (Old Rappahannock County Wills 1682-1687: 23) (1684)
Pusamuck (Old Rappahannock County Orders 1686-1692:324) (1692)
Pewmondsend (PB 9:80) (1697)
Powomasend (PB 9:80) (1697)
Powomasend (Essex County Deeds and Wills 1695-1699:165) (1697)
Pewmansend (Essex County Deeds and Wills 1695-1699:165) (1697)
Pewamanesee (PB 9:616) (1704)
Pewmansend (PB 10:452) (1719)
Nusensend (PB 10:249) (1725)

Peumansend (PB 13:338) (1728)
Pumondsend (PB 13:377) (1728)
Pewmanzens (PB 27:399) (1749)
Pumansend (Fry-Jefferson map) (1751)

PHOTOMOKE

Creek: Northumberland County; a tributary of Lower Machodoc Creek, which is on the Potomac River's right side.

Photomoke (Northumberland County Deeds and Orders 1650-1652:50) (1650)

PIANKATANK

Bay: Mathews and Middlesex Counties; at the intersection of the Piankatank River and Chesapeake Bay.

Payankatank (CJS I:53) (1607)
Pyankatank (CJS I:229) (1608)
Pyankatanck (PB 1:805) (1642)
Peankatanck (PB 1:824) (1642)
Pyancke (PB 3:130) (1652)
Pyanck (PB 3:224) (1653)

Creek: King and Queen County; on the York River's left side; upstream from the Poropotank River.

Peanckatancke (PB 1:829) (1642)

Ferry: Middlesex and Gloucester Counties; a ferry crossing below Dragon Swamp.

Pyanketanke (Middlesex County Order Book 1673-1680:85) (1678)

Indian Town: Middlesex County; in the immediate vicinity of Piankatank Shores and Woodstock.

Payank (Zuniga map) (1608)

Powhatan Indian Place Names in Tidewater Virginia

Payankatank (CJS I:53) (1608)
Parankatank (Smith map) (1612)
Peancketancke (PB 5:396) (1663)

Parish: Lancaster County; formed in 1657 when the county was divided into two parishes. Piankatank Parish, on the Rappahannock River's right side, became extinct in 1667 when Christ Church Parish was formed (DVA 152-153; JHB 1660-1693:35; HEN II:252).

Place: Mathews and Middlesex Counties; in the territory adjoining the Piankatank River.

Peganketanke (PB 2:302) (1651)

River: the boundary separating Gloucester and Mathews Counties from Middlesex County; tributary of the Chesapeake Bay; the river's headwaters form Dragon Swamp.

Payankatank (CJS I:53) (1608)
Payankatanke (CJS II:147) (1612)
Peanckatancke (PB 1:798) (1642)
Pyankatanke (PB 1:803) (1642)
Pyankatanck (PB 1:805) (1642)
Pyanketancke (PB 1:805) (1642)
Peankatanke (PB 1:870) (1642)
Peanketanke (PB 2:165) (1648)
Peanketank (PB 2:196) (1649)
Pyanketanck (PB 3:32) (1652)
Peyanketank (PB 3:116) (1652)
Pyanketanke (PB 3:6) (1653)
Pieanketank (PB 3:44) (1653)
Piankatank (PB 3:46) (1653)
Peyanketanke (PB 3:224) (1653)
Pyanketank (PB 3:269) (1654)
Peanketanke (PB 3:384) (1655)
Peanketancke (PB 4:59) (1656)
Pyancketanck (PB 4:127) (1663)
Peankatank (Old Rappahannock County Record Book 1656-1664:319) (1663)
Peancketanck (PB 4:134) (1664)
Peancketank (PB 5:506) (1665)
Pieanketanck (PB 6:490) (1673)
Peanketanck (Middlesex County Order Book 1673-1680:37) (1675)
Poyanketanke (PB 7:618) (1687)
Peanketanck (PB 8:208) (1691)
Piankatank (Fry-Jefferson map) (1751)

Swamp: the boundary between King and Queen County and Middlesex and Essex Counties; headwaters of the Piankatank River; now called Dragon Swamp or Run.

Pyanketanke (PB 4:29) (1656)
Peanketanke (PB 4:30) (1656)
Peanketanck (PB 4:146) (1657)
Peancketanck (PB 4:289) (1660)
Peanketan (PB 4:46) (1662)
Peancketancke (PB 5:176) (1663)
Pianketanke (PB 5:225) (1663)
Peanketank (PB 5:226) (1663)
Peanketank (PB 9:10) (1695)

PIPSCO

Bay: Surry County; on the James River's right side; upstream from Swanns Point.

Pipscoes (PB 1:629) (1636)

Place: Surry County; on the James River's right side, just west of Broad Swamp and west of Four Mile Tree; originally, the town of Indian leader Pipsco or Pepiscunimah.

Pipsco (HAILE 66) (1612)
Pipsico (PB 1:629) (1636)
Pipsco (Surry County Plat Book 2:18) (1879)

Powhatan Indian Place Names in Tidewater Virginia

PISCATAWAY

Creek and Swamp: Essex County; on the Rappahannock River's right side; downstream from Tappahannock.

Pascation (PB 3:81) (1652)
Puscacon (PB 3:119) (1652)
Puscation (PB 3:1) (1653)
Puscaticon (PB 3:21) (1653)
Puscaticond (PB 3:318) (1654)
Pashataquon (PB 4:45) 1656)
Paskato (PB 4:45) (1656)
Pasckataynon (PB 4:45) (1656)
Puscattecond (PB 4:234) (1658)
Puscattecon (PB 4:246) (1658)
Pascaticon (PB 4:301) (1661)
Pascatticon (PB 4:306) (1661)
Pascaton (PB 4:78) (1662)
Piscaticon (PB 4:312) (1662)
Purcaticon (PB 5:149) (1662)
Piscattaway (PB 5:241) (1663)
Pascataway (PB 5:147) (1664)
Piscaton (Old Rappahannock County Record Book 1656-1664:344) (1665)
Puscataway (Old Rappahannock County Record Book 1663-1668:276) (1667)
Puscatua (PB 6:319) (1670)
Pascattaway (Herrman map) (1670)
Puscatna (PB 6:371) (1671)
Puscatakon (PB 6:371) (1671)
Pascutway (PB 6:556) (1675)
Piscatisin (Old Rappahannock County Deeds and Wills 1677-1682:237) (1679)
Pescataway (Essex County Deeds and Wills 1692-1695:62-63) (1690)
Pescattaway (PB 8:198) (1691)
Pescataway (PB 8:210) (1691)
Pescatacon (Essex County Deeds and Wills 1692-1695:114-115) (1692)
Pescatoway (PB 9:110) (1697)
Pascatacon (Essex County Deeds and Wills 1699-1702:4) (1699)
Pisscuttawaya (Essex County Deeds and Wills 1699-1702:4) (1699)

Piscataway (Jefferson-Brooke map) (1747)

Place: Essex County; in the vicinity of Piscataway Creek.

Pescation (Old Rappahannock County Record Book 1656-1664:233) (1662)
Piscaticow (Old Rappahannock County Record Book 1656-1664:262) (1663)

Neck: Stafford County; on the Potomac River's right bank; on the Aquia Creek's left side; the neck of land terminating in Brent Point.

Puscataway (PB 4:179) (1658)

PISSACOACK

Indian Town: Richmond County; on the Rappahannock River's left bank; near Smoots Landing and across from the lower end of Paynes Island.

Pissacoack (Smith map) (1612)
Pisacack (CJS III:174) (1624)
Pissaccoack (Ogilby map) (1676)

PISSASECK

Indian Town: Westmoreland County; on the Rappahannock River's left bank at Leedstown; a king's house.

Pissaseck (Smith map) (1612)
Pissasack (CJS III:174) (1624)
Pissassack (CJS III:177) (1624)

POCHICHERY

Neck: City of Norfolk, formerly Norfolk County; near the Lafayette River.

Pochichery (PB 4:25) (1655)

Powhatan Indian Place Names in Tidewater Virginia

POCHINK

Place: Stafford County; on the Potomac River's right side; on the Potomac Creek's left side.

Pochicck (PB 4:91) (1656)
Pochink (PB 4:91) (1656)

POCKATAMANIO

Run: King and Queen County; a small unnamed stream on the on the left side of the Mattaponi River near Walkerton. Edward Diggs' 1653 patent called Matapony Fort was located in this vicinity.

Pockatamanio (PB 3:16) (1653)
Potataweno (PB 5:503) (1665)
Potapannica (PB 7:559) (1687)

POCKASHOCK

Branch or Creek: Chesterfield County; on the right side of the James River; upstream side of Falling Creek, near Wilkinson Terrace.

Pockashock (William Byrd Title Book 93) (1696)
Pocoshock (PB 9:527) (1703)

POCOMOKE

Branch and Creek: Accomack County; Taylor Creek, a tributary of Pungoteague Creek.

Poccomoke (PB 3:123) (1652)
Pocomoke (PB 3:198) (1652)
Pocomock (PB 3:294) (1654)
Pocomeck (PB 3:332) (1655)

Bay or Sound: Accomack County, Virginia, and Somerset County, Maryland; a tributary of the Chesapeake Bay at the mouth of the Pocomoke River.

Pocomoke (Marzone map, 1855)

Place: Accomack County; in the vicinity of the Pocomoke River and Sound.

Pocamoke (PB 6:405) (1672)
Pokamock (PB 6:676) (1679)

River: Accomack County; a tributary of Pocomoke Sound and Chesapeake Bay.

Pohomoke (PB 5:219) (1662)
Pokomoke (PB 5:190) (1663)
Pokomock) (PB 5:183) (1664)
Pocomooc (PB 5:491) (1666)
Pocomook (PB 5:492) (1666)
Pocomooke (PB 5:494) (1666)
Pockomoke (PB 6:78) (1667)
Pokeamoke (PB 6:402) (1672)
Pokomoack (Herrman map) (1670)
Pokamoak (Northampton County Deeds, Wills, Etc. 1680-1692:42) (1679)
Pocomack (Northampton County Wills, Deeds, etc. 1711-1718:58) (1708)
Pocomock (Northampton County Wills, Deeds, etc. 1711-1718:58) (1708)
Pocamoak Northampton County Wills, Deeds, etc. 1711-1718:45) (1711)
Pokemoke (acc) 231(Northampton County Wills, Deeds, etc. 1718-1725:81) (1720)
Pockamock (Northampton County Wills, Deeds, etc. 1718-1725:171) (1723)

POHICK

Bay or Creek: Fairfax County; a tributary of Gunston Cove, Accotink

Powhatan Indian Place Names in Tidewater Virginia

Bay, and the Potomac River on its right side.

Pohinck (Westmoreland County, Deeds and Wills 1:32) (1656)
Pohick (PB 4:323) (1666)
Poehick (PB 6:244) (1669)

POKATINK

Swamp: Surry County; on the James River's right side; Moore's Swamp, a tributary of Lawnes Creek.

Poeaketinke (PB 6:281) (1669)
Pokatink (PB 7:184 (1682)
Pokotink (PB 7:247) (1683)

POPOEMAN

Creek: Essex County; a branch of Occupacia Creek.

Popoeman (Essex County (Essex County Deeds and Wills 1695-1699:53-54) (1696)

POPOMAR

Branch: Essex County; Handpole Creek on the left side of Occupacia Creek, which is a tributary of the Rappahannock River's right side.

Popomar (PB 9:597) (1704)

POQUOSON

Creek or River: the boundary between the town of Poquoson (originally York County) and the city of Hampton (formerly Elizabeth City County); later called the Old Poquoson, but is now known as the Northwest Branch of the Back River.

Pocoson (PB 1:156) (1634)
Poquoson (PB 1:317) (1635)
Poquosun (PB 1:201) (1635)
Old Pokosen (Herrman map) (1670)
Pocosin (Bache map) (1853-1854)
Poqhosan (Green map) (1862)
Poquosin (Bache map) (1862b)

Creek or River: the boundary between the town of Poquoson and York County; often called the New Poquoson; a tributary of the Chesapeake Bay.

Poquoson (PB 1:225) (1635)
New Pokosen (Herrman map) (1670)
New Pocoson (Fry-Jefferson map) (1751)
Pocosan (Anonymous map) (1776)
Poquoson (USGS Hampton quadrangle) (1906)

Parish: York County; established in 1635 and in 1692 became Charles Parish (DSVA 169-171).

Pecosan (PB 6:43) (1666)

Places: York County; on the right side of the York River's mouth; these marshy areas were variously called the Old Poquoson or the New Poquoson.

Poquoson (PB 1:582) (1638)
Paquosons (PB 5:336) (1663)

Pond: York County; head of the Poquoson River, which is a tributary of the Chesapeake Bay.

Pequoson (PB 4:75) (1662)

River: Northumberland County; on the Potomac River's right side.

Powhatan Indian Place Names in Tidewater Virginia

New Pocoson (Northumberland County Wills, Inventories &c. 1652-1658:127) (1657)

Swamp: a probable reference to the Dragon Swamp, which separates Middlesex and Gloucester Counties.

Pacoson (PB 4:278) (1659)

POROPOTANK

Creek: Gloucester County; on the York River's left side; now called Adams Creek, just east of the Poropotank River.

Little Portopotanck (Herrman map) (1670)

Creek or River: part of the boundary between Gloucester and King and Queen Counties; on the York River's left side.

Poruptank (Velasco map) (1610)
Poropotanck (PB 1:797) (1642)
Porepotanke (PB 1:806) (1642)
Poropotanke (PB 2:192) (1649)
Porropotank (PB 3:203) (1652)
Poropotancke (PB 3:8) (1653)
Poropetanke (PB 3:322) (1654)
Peropatanck (Northumberland County Record Book 1658-1662:5) (1654)
Porotank (PB 3:382) (1656)
Poropotank (Langston map) (1662)
Portopotanck (Herrman map) (1670)
Porpotancke (PB 6:442) (1672)
Pocopotank (CO 1/22 ff 155-156) (1668)
Pourtopotank (PB 14:300) (1731)
Potopotank (Bache map) (1857-1858)

Indian Town: Gloucester County; on the York River's left side; upstream from the Poropotank River's mouth.

Poruptanck (Smith map) (1612)

Swamp: Gloucester and King and Queen Counties; on the York River's left side; at the head of one of main branches of the Poropotank River.

Poropotank (PB 2:338) (1651)
Propotanck (PB 3:309) (1654)
Propotanke (PB 3:309) (1654)
Poropotanke (PB 4:56) (1656)
Poropotancke (PB 5:353) (1662)
Tanks Poropotank (PB 6:151) (1665)
Tannspotopotank (Franklin map, 1885b)

PORTOBAGO

Bay: Caroline County; on the Rappahannock River's right side, upstream from Marsh Point and downstream from Peumansend Creek.

Portobego (Old Rappahannock County Deeds and Wills 1656-1664:322) (1663)
Portobacco (PB 9:594) (1704)
Port Tobago (Bache map) (1854)

Creek and Swamp: Caroline County; on the Rappahannock River's right side; a tributary of Portobago Bay.

Potobaco (PB 5:396) (1665)
Potobacco (PB 6:62) (1667)
Porotobacco (Herrman map) (1670)
Pooretobacco (Essex County Deeds and Wills 1695-1699:233) (1693)
Pooretobacco (Essex County Deeds and Wills 1692-1695:382) (1693)
Portobayoe (Essex County Deeds and Wills 1695-1699:165) (1697)
Poretobacco (Essex County, Deeds 13:258) (1709)
Portobago (Essex County, Deeds 13:433) (1711)
Portobago (Jefferson-Brooke map) (1747)
Port Tobacco (Fry-Jefferson map) (1751)

Powhatan Indian Place Names in Tidewater Virginia

Indian Town: Caroline County; on the east side of Portobago Bay; upstream from the site of an earlier village, Nandtanghtacund. In 1677, a chief named Pattanochus signed the Treaty of Middle Plantation on their behalf (PP 120).

Portobaccoe (PB 4:10) (1655)
Port Tobacco (PB 4:43) (1656)
Poretobacco (PB 5:317) (1662)
Potobacco (PB 5:412) (1663)
Potobaco (PB 6:61) (1667)
Potobago (Old Rappahannock County, Deeds 5:491) (1674)
Port Tobago (BEV 184) (1704)

Path: Essex County; path paralleling the Rappahannock River's right side.
Potobacco (PB 5:397) (1665)
Portobacco (PB 6:13) (1666)

POTANK

Creek: Westmoreland County; on the Potomac River's right side; across Coles Neck from Lower Machodoc Creek; probably Gardner Creek.

Potank (Jefferson-Brooke map) (1747)

POTAUNCAC

Indian Town: New Kent County; on the Pamunkey River's right side; in the vicinity of Cousaic Marsh. In ca. 1610, Essenetaugh was the chief in this town (HAILE 628).

Potawuncack (Zuniga map) (1608)
Potauacao (Smith map) (1612)
Pataunck (HAILE 628) (1612)
Potauncac (CJS II:255) (1612)
Potauncak (CJS III:205) (1624)

POTNICK

Creek: Fairfax County; on the Potomac River's right side; a branch of Accotink Creek, which is tributary to Gunston Cove.

Potnick (Jefferson-Brooke map) (1747)

POTOBACK

Place: Surry County; on the James River's right side; upstream from Lower Chippokes Creek's west side.

Potoback (PB 1:855) (1642)
Pacotacke (PB 2:161) (1649)

POTOMAC

Creek: King George (formerly Westmoreland) County; on the Potomac River's right side; part of the boundary between King George and Stafford Counties.

Potomeck (PB 2:333) (1651)
Petomack (PB 3:273) (1654)
Pecomeck (PB 3:297) (1654)
Potomake (PB 4:46) (1656)
Patomeck (PB 4:222) (1658)
Poteseck (PB 4:80) (1662)
Patomacke (PB 5:295) (1662)
Potomack (PB 5:421) (1665)
Potoamack (PB 6:309) (1669)
Patomoack (Herrman map) (1670)
Pottomack (Stafford County Record Book 1686-1693:44) (1687)
Patowmack (Fry-Jefferson map) (1751)
Potowmack (Tatham map) (1813)
Potomac (Boye map) (1826)

Indian Town: Stafford County; on the Potomac River's right side; on Marlboro Point, at Potomac Creek's mouth; a king's house. The name of the tribe's chief, brother of Iopassus (Japazaws), was never recorded; in 1662, the chief's name was Wahanganoche (PP 94, 121).

Pataromerke (CJS I:55) (1608)
Patomeck (HAILE 485) (1610)
Patowomeck (HAILE 485) (1610)
Patawomeck (Velasco map) (1610)
Patawomeck (Smith map) (1612)
Patawomeck (Smith map) (1612)
Potowmack (HEN II:149) (1662)
Potowmeck (HEN II:150) (1662)

Path: King George County; leading to the Patawomeck Indian town.

Patomack (PB 5:389) (1664)

River: the boundary between Virginia and Maryland; a tributary of the Chesapeake Bay.

Patawomeck (HAILE 45) (1612)
Pattawomeck (HAILE:107) (1612)
Patawomecke (CJS II:277) (1612)
Patawomeke (CJS II:142) (1612)
Pataomecke (HAILE 800) (1614)
Patawomeake (CJS:III: 243) (1624)
Potomeck (PB 2:186) (1649)
Potomock (PB 2:225) (1650)
Potomecke (PB 2:246) (1650)
Pataomak (Farrer map) (1651)
Pattomake (PB 4:83) (1651)
Potomacke (Northumberland County Wills and Inventories 1652-1658:2) (1651)
Patowmack (PB 3:38) (1653)
Potemeck (PB 3:275) (1654)
Patomacke (PB 5:295) (1654)
Peetomake (PB 4:70) (1654)
Petomack (PB 4:273) (1654)
Petomeck (PB 3:283) (1654)
Petomecke (PB 4:5) (1655)
Potewmacke (PB 4:50) (1656)
Pattewmacke (PB 4:68) (1656)
Potomake (PB 4:67) (1656)
Petowmack (PB 4:71) (1656)
Pattewmacke (PB 4:68) (1656)
Patomek (PB 4:95) (1657)
Patomeck (PB 4:104) (1657)
Petomake (PB 4:78) (1662)
Patomecke (PB 4:303) (1662)
Petomeke (PB 5:283) (1663)
Patomeke (PB 5:216) (1663)
Patomick (Stafford County Court Book 1664-1669, 1689-1693:10) (1664)
Potomok (Pargellis, "An Account of the Indians," 239) (1688)
Potomack (Fry-Jefferson map) (1751)
Petomeck (Northumberland County Order Book 1666-1678:344) (1678)
Potowmack (Madison map) (1807)
Potomac (Boye map) 1826)

POTTACOCOCK

Place: New Kent County; on the Chickahominy River's left side; probably in the vicinity of Turner Neck.

Pottacocock (PB 1:641) (1639)

POWAKEI

Swamp: King and Queen County; on the Mattaponi River's left side; near Walkerton; probably Clark Swamp.

Powakei (PB 5:139) (1663)

POWCOMONET

Indian Town: Richmond County; on the Rappahannock River's left side; east side of Richardson Creek.

Powcomonet (Smith map) (1612)

Powhatan Indian Place Names in Tidewater Virginia

POWETRIDGE

Creek: King George County; on the Rappahannock River's left side; now known as Jetts Creek.

Porortridge (PB 5:168) (1662)
Powetridge (PB 5:168) (1664)

POWHATAN

Bay: Gloucester County; on the York River's left side; now known as Purton Bay; downstream from the Poropotank River.

Purton (PB 5:470) (1666)
Porton (Herrman map) (1670)
Portan (Fry-Jefferson map) 1751
Purton (Franklin map) (1885b)

Branch, Creek, and Swamp: James City County; on the James River's left side; joins the river at the western end of Jamestown Island.

Powhetan (PB 1:108) (1631)
Powehetan (PB 2:48) (1646)
Poetan (PB 2:129) (1648)
Powatan (PB 2:270) (1650)
Powetan (PB 3:225) (1653)
Powhitan (PB 4:62) (1656)
Pohatan (PB 4:219) (1658)
Pohetan (PB 4:267) (1659)
Porohatan (PB 8:149) (1691)
Powehatan (PB 8:146) (1691)
Powhatan (Fry-Jefferson map) (1751)
Portan (Anonymous map) (1776)
Purtan (Bache map) (1857-1858)

Bridge: James City County; a bridge across Powhatan Creek or Swamp.

Powhetan (PB 1:905) (1643)
Poetan (PB 5:348) (1662)

Creek: Gloucester County; a tributary of Purtan Bay on the York River's left side; farthest up the York of the three creeks flowing into that bay.

Purton (PB 5:470) (1666)

Indian Town: City of Richmond (formerly Henrico County); on the James River's left side near Shockoe Creek. In 1607, this frontier town was ruled by Parahunt, a son of the great chief Powhatan (PP 33, 52).

Pawatahs Towre (HAILE 106) (1607)
Pohatans Towre (TYLER 141) (1607)
Poetan (Tyndall map) (1608)
Powatan (Velasco map) (1610)
Powhatan (Vingboons map) (1639)

Path: Gloucester County; trail probably leading to Purtan Bay and Werowocomoco.

Purton (PB 5:174) (1664)

Place: City of Richmond (formerly Henrico County); on the James River's left side, near Stony, Powhite, and Reedy Creeks.

Pohatan (William Byrd Title Book 85) (1710)
Powhatan (Captaine map) (1781)

Place: James City County; land at the head of Powhatan Creek.

Poetan (Robinson Family Papers II:37) (1684)
Powhatan (Anonymous map) (1776)

Pond: James City County; at the head of Powhatan Creek.

Poetan (PB 3:304) (1654)

Powhatan Indian Place Names in Tidewater Virginia

River: original name of the James River, along which Chief Powhatan's home town was the most prominent.

Powahtan (HAILE 482) (1610)
Powhatan (HAILE 602) (1612)

Tree: Henrico County; vicinity of Three Mile Creek.

Powhetans (PB 1:148) (1634)

POWHITE

Creek: Chesterfield County; on the James River's right side; near Bon Air and the Willow Oaks Country Club.

Powhite (PB 7:547) (1687)

Creek: Hanover County; on the Chickahominy Swamp's left side near Cold Harbor.

Powhite (Captaine map) (1781)

Indian Town: City of Richmond; on the James River's left side; near Shockoe Creek. "Powhite" is a corruption of "Powhatan."

Powhite (William Byrd Title Book 103) (1663)

Path: New Kent County; on the Chickahominy Swamp's left side.

Powhite (PB 6:499) (1661)

Swamp: Chesterfield County; on the James River's right side; head of Powhite Creek.

Powhite (PB 8:53) (1693)

Swamp: Hanover County; on the Chickahominy Swamp's left side.

Powhite (PB 4:470) (1661)

POYEKTANK

Indian Town: Richmond County; on the Rappahannock River's left side; west of Wellfords Wharf.

Poyektank (Smith map) (1612)

POYKEMKACK

Indian Town: Richmond County; north of Little Carter Creek's midpoint.

Poykemkack (Smith map) (1612)

PUNGOTEAGUE

Branch: Accomack County; on Nasswaddox Creek's right side; now called Church Creek.

Pungoteke (Northampton County, Deeds and Wills 4:125) (1651)

Creek or River: Accomack County; a tributary of the Chesapeake Bay.

Pungotege (PB 3:105) (1652)
Pongotege (PB 3:121) (1652)
Pongotegue (PB 3:127) (1652)
Pungotegge (Northampton County, Deeds and Wills 4: 90) (1652)
Pongoteage (PB 3:12) (1654)
Pungotegue (PB 3:339) (1655)
Pungoteage (PB 4:2) (1655)
Pungoteague (PB 5:541) (1661)
Punkoteak (Herrman map) (1670)

Powhatan Indian Place Names in Tidewater Virginia

Pungateage (PB 6:373) (1671)
Pungatege Creek (PB 9:136) (1698)
Pongoteague (Marzone map) (1855)

Indian Town: Accomack County; on Pungoteague Creek's left side; in Sluitkill Neck.

Pungoteague (PB 4:9) (1655)
Pongoteige (PB 6:638) (1678)
Pungotege (Anonymous 1894:363) (1702)
Pungoteque (BEV 184) (1704)

Place: Accomack County; area on Pungoteague Creek's right side.

Pungat (PB 6:460) (1673)

PUTANAK

Creek: James City and York Counties; on the York River's right side; probably in the vicinity of Skimino Creek.

Putanak (PB 1:863) (1642)

QUACKCOHOWAON

Indian town: King William County; on the Mattaponi River's right bank; in the vicinity of Horse Landing.

Quaconamaock (Zuniga map) (1608)
Quackcohowaon (Smith map) (1612)
Quaynohomock (EJC I:320) (1694)

QUANTICO

Creek: Prince William County; on the Potomac River's right bank.
Quancico (PB 3:275) (1654)

Quanticott (PB 3:312) (1654)
Quantecot (PB 4:159) (1657)
Quanticoke (PB 5:363) (1664)
Quanticutt (PB 5:465) (1665)
Quantiqunt (PB 6:348) (1671)
Quanticock (PB 6:619) (1677)
Quantico (Fry-Jefferson map) (1751)

QUEENS

Creek: York County; a tributary on the York River's right side; the eastern branch is now known as Cheatham Pond.

Queens (PB 1:62) (1637)

Creek: Charles City County; a tributary on the James River's left side.

Queens (PB 1:445) (1651)

Creek: Mathews (formerly Gloucester) County; a tributary on the Piankatank River's right side, by means of Hills Bay.

Queens (PB 3:5) (1653)

QUEENS GRAVE
Creek: City of Norfolk (formerly Norfolk County); a tributary of the Lafayette River, which until the early 20th century was known as Tanner's Creek; the Lafayette River is a tributary of the Elizabeth River's right side.

Queens Grave (PB 1:285) (1653)

QUIACOMACK

Neck: Lancaster County; on the left side of the Corrotoman River's mouth; in the environs of Corotoman Point.

Quicomack (PB 2:308) (1650)
Quiacomack (PB 3:367) (1655)

Powhatan Indian Place Names in Tidewater Virginia

Quiacomico (PB 5:136) (1662)
Quiaccomake (PB 5:198) (1663)

QUICHECOHANEK

Place: Northumberland County; on the Potomac River's right bank; a small neck of land between Bridgeman Creek and Fountain Cove, which are branches of Hull Creek.

Quichecohanek (Northumberland County Record Book 1650-1652:62) (1650)

QUIETJANJECK

Place: Accomack County; on the left bank of Onancock Creek.

Quietjanjeck (Accomack County, Deeds and Wills 1663-1666:40) (1663)

QUIOCCASIN

Creek: Essex County; ultimately a tributary on the Rappahannock River's right bank; in the headwaters of Broad Creek and above Blandfield Point; not found in records prior to the mid-20th century.
Place: Essex County; the site of a house or mortuary temple located on the Mattaponi Indians' land near the head of Piscataway Creek. "Quioccasin" meant "temple" in the Powhatan language.

Quioquesen (Old Rappahannock County Record Book 1[1656-1664]:111) (1660)
Quiouhise (Old Rappahannock County Record Book 1[1656-1664]:249-250) (1661)

Point: Essex County; on the Rappahannock River's right bank; near the mouth of Broad Creek; possibly Blandfield Point.

Quioquinson (Old Rappahannock County Records 1[1656-1664]:192-193) (1663)
Quiocison (PB 10:14) (1714).

QUIOKSA

Branch: Northumberland County; a branch of Presley (formerly Chingegan) Creek; a tributary of the Potomac River's right side.

Quioksa (PB 2:186) (1649)

QUIRANK

Place: the Powhatan Indian name for the Blue Ridge Mountains.

Quirank (HAILE 103) (1607)

QUIOXTERS

Branch: Northumberland County; in the vicinity of the Coan River.

Quioxters (PB 6:11)

QUIRUCK

Point: Caroline County; on the Rappahannock River' right bank; on the upstream side of Goldenvale Creek's mouth.

Quiruck (or Quiunck) (PB 6:7) (1666)

QUIYOUGHCOHANNOCK

Indian Town: Surry County; on the right bank of Upper Chippokes Creek, a tributary of the James River's right side; a king's house. Before ca. 1610, the

Powhatan Indian Place Names in Tidewater Virginia

chief was Pepiscunimah (Pipsco); after his deposition, Oholasc ruled as regent for her son, Tatahcoope, rumored to be a son of the great chief Powhatan. A petty chief under them was Chopoke (source of place name Chippokes) (HAILE 621; PP 51, 58n.).

Quiyoughcohannock (Smith map) (1612)
Quayoughcohanck (Velasco map) (1610)
Quiyoughcohanocke (CJS II:146) (1612)
Quiyoughquohanock (CJS II:266) (1612)
Coiacohhanauke (HAILE 622) (1612)
Quiyoughcohanock (HAILE 622) (1612)
Quyyoughcahanock (HAILE 655) (1612)
Quiyoughcohanock (Vingboons map) (1639)
Quiyonghcohanock (Ogilby map) (1676)

QUOSAUGH

Indian Town: New Kent County; on the Chickahominy River's left bank; above Rumley Marsh and Turner Neck.

Quosaugh (Zuniga map) (1610)

RAMAGSTUCK

Place: Accomack County; somewhere north of Onancock Creek, a tributary of the Chesapeake Bay.

Romagstuck (PB 6:493) (1673)
Ramagstuck (Accomack County, Wills 1673-1676:344) (1675)

RAPPAHANNOCK

Bay: Lancaster and Middlesex Counties; old name for the Rappahannock River's broad mouth.

Rappahannocke (PB 1:865) (1642)

Creek: Richmond and Westmoreland Counties; a tributary on the Rappahannock River's left side; now known as Cat Point Creek.

Great Rappahannock (PB 3:357) (1655)
Great Rapahack (PB 4:5) (1655)
Rappahanock Main (PB 5:154) (1663)
Rappahanack (Fry-Jefferson map) (1751)
Rappahannock (Anonymous map) (1776)

Creek: Surry County; on the James River's right side; now known as Crouch Creek.

Tappahannock (PB 1:604) (1638)
Tapahanock (PB 3:222) (1653)
Rappahannah (PB 7:67) (1680)

Indian Town: Richmond County; on the right bank of Little Carter Creek, a tributary to the Rappahannock River's left side; a king's house. In 1651, the chief's name was Accopatough; after his death that year, his successor was Taweeren, followed by Wachicopa in 1658 (PP 118).

Topahanocke (CJS I:51) (1608)
Tapohanock (CJS I:53) (1608)
Toppohanock (Zuniga map) (1608)
Topahanock (Velasco map) (1610)
Toppahannock (Smith map) (1612)
Tapahatonahs (VCR IV:9) (1623)
Rapahanock (CJS III:177) (1624)

Marsh: Surry County; on the James River's right bank; now called Kennon Marsh.

Tapahanna (PB 1:206) (1635)
Taphanna (PB 2:94) (1646)
Tappahanna (PB 1:415) (1636)

Powhatan Indian Place Names in Tidewater Virginia

Tappahanoc (Reid map) (1776)
Tappahanock (Fry-Jefferson map) (1751)
Toppahanock (Henry map) (1770)
Tappahanock (Captaine map) (1781)

Path: Middle Peninsula and Northern Neck; a series of trails running from the York River's left bank to the Rappahannock River's right bank and beyond.

Rappahannock (PB 3:90) (1653)
Rapahanock (PB 6:84) (1667)

Place: Surry County; on the James River's right bank; in the vicinity of Claremont.

Tapahanauk (HAILE 117) (1607)
Rapahanna (HAILE 92) (1608)
Tapahanagh (HAILE 184) (1608)
Tapahanah (HAILE 185) (1608)
Tappahanocke (CJS I:31) (1608)
Topohanack (CJS I:37) (1608)
Topahanock (Zuniga map) (1608)
Topahonno (Tyndall map) (1608)
Tapahanock (HAILE 622) (1612)
Rappahannock (HAILE 608) (1612)
Tappahannah (PB 1:53) (1627)
Tappahanna (PB 1:880) (1643)

Point: Lancaster County; on the left bank of the Rappahannock River's junction with the Chesapeake Bay; at the tip of Fleets Island; since 1650 called Windmill Point (PB 2:226).

Rappahannock (PB 2:226) (1650)

River: the boundary between the Middle Peninsula and the Northern Neck; a tributary of the Chesapeake Bay.

Topahanock (CJS I:51) (1608)
Topahanocke (CJS :I:51) (1608)

Toppahanock (Smith map) (1612)
Toppahannock (CJS II:228) (1612)
Topahanah (HAILE 800) (1614)
Rappahanock (Herrman map) (1670)
Rapohanock (Pargellis, "An Account of the Indians," 239) (1688)
Tappahamock (Jefferson-Brooke map) (1747)
Rappahannock (Bache map) (1851-1856)
Tappahannock (Gilmer map) (1864a)

RAPTESTANK

Place: King William County; a neck of land at the confluence of the Pamunkey and Mattaponi Rivers; later known as Pamunkey Neck.

Raptestank (Velasco map) (1610)

RAQUETO

Branch: King and Queen County; a tributary on the Mattaponi River's left bank; close to the Peptico (Popetyke) Branch of Goalders Creek and the old Chiskiack Indian path leading toward the Piankatank River.

Raqueto (PB 5:311) (1664)

RASSAWEK

Indian Town: Fluvanna County; at the junction of the James and Rivanna Rivers, near Columbia; at Point of Fork; a king's house. Occupied by Monacan Indians, the name is Siouan rather than Algonquian.

Rasawek (CJS I:46) (1608)
Rasaweck (CJS I:51) (1608)
Rasawrack (HAILE 159) (1608)
Rassaweck (Zuniga map) (1608)
Rossawick (Velasco map, 1611)

Powhatan Indian Place Names in Tidewater Virginia

Rassawek (Smith map) (1612)
Rasseweac (CJS II:253) (1612)
Rassasock (Vingboons map) (1639)

RHOTANOKE

Neck: Westmoreland County; between two branches of the Yeocomico River.

Rhotanoke (Northumberland County, Deeds and Wills 1650-1652:50) (1651)

RICKAHOCK

Creek: James City County; a tributary, now known as Mill Creek, of Diascund Creek, itself a tributary on the Chickahominy River's left bank.

Richahocke (PB 4:55) (1656)
Rochohock (PB 4:175) (1658)
Rockahock (Patterson map) (1873-1874)

Indian Town: Charles City County; on the Chickahominy River's right bank; near Cypress Bank.

Roghtacut (Zuniga map) (1608)
Righkahauke (Smith map) (1612)

Indian Town: New Kent County; on the Pamunkey River's right bank, between Black and Big Creeks (see **Place**, below).

Righkahauck (CJS I:41) (1608)

Indian Town: King and Queen County; on the Mattaponi River's left bank at Rickahock.

Rickahock (EJC:I:320; CSP I:22) (1689)

Indian Town: City of Chesapeake or City of Suffolk; somewhere between the Elizabeth and Nansemond Rivers.

Rickahake (CJS III:291) (1624)

Path: James City, York, and New Kent and York Counties; paralleled the right bank of the York River, passing close to the Chickahominy River.

Richahock (PB 2:264) (1650)
Ricahoc (PB 2:321) (1651)
Ricohock (PB 3:1) (1653)
Ricohoake (PB 3:5) (1653)
Ricohack (PB 3:54) (1653)
Rickohauke (PB 3:8) (1654)
Richohock (PB 3:263) (1654)
Richahocke (PB 4:55) (1656)
Rickahock (PB 4:110) (1657)
Rockahock (PB 4:281) (1661)
Rockahoe (PB 5:354) 1662)
Rickahoc (PB 5:452) (1665)
Richahoc (PB 7:44) (1680)
Roccohock (PB 7:67) (1680)
Rickahack (PB 7:221) (1682)

Place: New Kent County; on the Pamunkey River's right bank; between Black and Big Creeks; the area near Rockahock Bar.

Rickahock (Langston map) (1662)
Rockahockaw (PB 5:195) (1664)

Place: New Kent County; on the Chickahominy River's left bank; above Turner Neck; across from Mattahunk Neck.

Richahocke (PB 4:55) (1656)
Rickahock (PB 4:110) (1657)

Powhatan Indian Place Names in Tidewater Virginia

Place: King and Queen County; on the Mattaponi River's left bank; upstream from Garnetts Creek; name still in use.

Ricahock (PB 2:195) (1649)
Rickohocke (PB 3:211) (1653)
Rocahock (PB 3:191) (1653)
Rickahock (USGS New Kent quadrangle) (1918)

Place: City of Alexandria (formerly part of Westmoreland and Fairfax Counties); on the Potomac River's right bank; above Hunting Creek.

Ricohockian Stand (PB 3:373) (1654)
Richahockian Stands (PB 4:304) (1662)

RICKENAW

Creek: King and Queen County; a tributary of Chapel Hill Creek, which flows into the Mattaponi River on its left side; close to the head of Piscataway Creek (a tributary of the Rappahannock River), where an Indian Town was located in the early 1660s and 1670s.

Rickenaw (USGS Aylett quadrangle) (1917)

ROATANK

Creek: Northumberland County; a tributary on the Potomac River's right side; downstream from the Yeocomico River; in the vicinity of Cherry Point Neck.

Roatank (PB 5:415) (1665)
Roatanke (PB 6:156) (1668)

ROHOWICK

Creek, Run, and Swamp: part of the boundary between Dinwiddie County and the City of Petersburg; on the Appomattox River's right bank; now known as Indian Town Creek and Cattail Run.

Ronhorak PB 7:45) (1680)
Rehowick (PB 8:38) (1690)
Rohoick (PB 9:149) (1698)
Rohowicke (PB 9:163) (1698)
Rohowick (PB 14:344) (1731)

Place: in the vicinity of the boundary between Dinwiddie County and the City of Petersburg; on the Appomattox River's right bank; near Indian Town Run.

Rehoweck (PB 8:38) (1690)
Rahowick (PB 8:77) (1690)
Rhohoick (Bristol Parish Vestry Book 35) (1727)

ROMANCOKE

Place: King William County; on the Pamunkey River's left bank; above West Point and across from Hill Marsh.

Candaungack (MCGC 482) (164[-])
Ramonak (HEN I:380) (1653)
Ramongack (PB 4:145) (1657)
Ramounca (Langston map) ([1662])
Romuncock (Fry-Jefferson map) (1751)
Woromankoke (William Black manuscript) (1774)
Romancoke (Anonymous plat) (1797)

ROWANTY

Creek and Swamp: Sussex and Dinwiddie Counties (formerly Surry County); a tributary on the Nottoway River's left side; Interstate 95 crosses it just north of Interchange 33. The name

Powhatan Indian Place Names in Tidewater Virginia

could be either Algonquian or Iroquoian, since tribes from both language families lived on it during the 17th century.

Rowanty (PB 9:714) (1706)
Rovanty (PB 14:414) (1732)
Rowanty (Boye map) (1826)

SAPPONY

Creek: Sussex and Dinwiddie Counties (formerly Surry County); on the right side of Stony Creek, a tributary of the Nottoway River.

Sappony (PB 10:265) (1715)
Sapone (PB 10:39) (1720)
Sapponey (Bristol Parish Vestry Book 114) (1727)

Creek: Chesterfield (formerly Henrico) County; tributary on the left side of the Appomattox River; the headwaters of the creek's left fork are near Skinquarter, on U.S. 360; name still in use.

Sapponey (PB 10:162) (1714)

Ford: Chesterfield (formerly Henrico) County; on the left side of the Appomattox River; in the vicinity of Bevil's (Beavil's) Bridge, which was near the Old Sappony Indian Town.

Sappony (PB 11:36) (1720)

Indian Town: Chesterfield (formerly Henrico) County; on the Appomattox River's left bank; close to the river and extending along Sapony Creek; a short distance upstream from Bevil's Bridge.

Sapponey (PB 10:162) (1714)
Sapony (PB 10:321) (1717)
Old Sappony (PB 11:36) (1720)

SCHIMINOE

Creek: New Kent County; a tributary on the Chickahominy River's left bank; crosses U.S. 60 northwest of Providence Forge.

Skennow (PB 4:49) (1656)
Skiminoe (PB 4:151) (1657)
Muskemino (PB 5:251) (1665)
Musciminoe (PB 6:229) (1669)

SEACOCK

Swamp: Southampton (formerly Isle of Wight) County; on the Blackwater River's left bank near Unity.

Seacock (PB 9:328) (1701)
Secauris (PB 10:176) (1720)
Seacawris (PB 11:271) (1723)
Scacawris (PB 12:104) (1724)

SECOBECK

Indian Town: Caroline County; on the Rappahannock River's right bank; in Moss Neck; below Dicks Creek.

Secobeck (Velasco map) 1611)
Secobeck (Smith map) (1612)
Secobbeck (Ogilby map) (1676)

SHAMAPINT

Indian Town: New Kent County; on the Pamunkey River's right bank; upstream from the mouth of Black Creek. In ca. 1610, Nansuapunck was the chief in this town (HAILE 628).

Powhatan Indian Place Names in Tidewater Virginia

Shamapint (Zuniga map, 1608)
Shamapa (HAILE 628) (1612)

SHOCCOE

Creek: City of Richmond; on the James River's bank; known today as Shoccoe Slip.

Chyinek (William Byrd Title Book 103) (1663)
Shaccoe William Byrd Title Book 103 (1663)
Shoccores (PB6:604) (1676)
Shacko (PB 7:548) (1687)
Shockhow (PB 605) (1687)
Shacco (William Byrd Correspondence I:389) (1729)
Shokoes (William Byrd Correspondence II:680) (1759)

Place: City of Richmond; plantation on which the Powite Indians were living in 1663. According William Byrd I, "Shaccoe Creek [was] formerly called Chyinak."

Shaccoe (William Byrd Title Book, 103) (1663)

SKICOAK

Indian Town: City of Portsmouth (formerly Norfolk County); somewhere west of the Elizabeth River; now part of an urbanized area.

Skicoak (de Bry 1590)

SKIMINO

Creek and Swamp: part of the boundary between York and James City Counties; a tributary on the York River's right side; the western boundary of Camp Peary.

Kimeno (PB 2:317) (1651)
Skimeno (PB 2:317) (1651)
Skimmino (PB 3:104) (1652)
Skiminoe (PB 3:115) (1652)
Skemino (PB 3:274) (1654)
Skemeno (PB 3:354) (1655)
Skemenoe (PB 3:358) (1655)
Skimino (PB 4:84) (1662)
Muskiminoughk (Langston map) (1662)
Scimmino (Fry-Jefferson map, 1751)
Simmino (Anonymous map) (1776)
Skimming (Bache map) (1857-1858)

Place: York County; area on the downstream side of Skimino Creek; on the York River's right bank.

Skemeno (PB 3:368) (1654)
Skimenoe (PB 4:12) (1655)
Skimino (PB 4:84) (1662)
Skiminoe (PB 5:243) (1662)

SOCKOBECK

Indian Town: King George County; on the Rappahannock River's left bank; near Popcastle Creek; across from Skinkers Neck.

Socobeck (Velasco map) (1610)
Sockobeck (Smith map) (1612)

SUSQUEHANNAH

Branch and Swamp: Southampton (formerly Isle of Wight) County; between the Blackwater and Nottoway Rivers.

Susquehannah (PB 12:81) (1724)
Suscahannah (PB 22:585) (1745)

Powhatan Indian Place Names in Tidewater Virginia

SWANSICUTT

Creek: Accomack County; a tributary of Chincoteague Bay that crosses the modern Virginia Maryland border; on the seaside; now Anglicized to Swans Gut Creek.

Swansicutts (PB 5:183) (1664)
Swanscutt (PB 6:265) (1669)
Swansecut (Herrman map) (1670)
Swansine (PB 6:392) (1671)
Swans (USCS map) (1858)
Swans Gut (D of C map) (1908)

TACOPACON

Spring: Westmoreland and Richmond Counties; on the Rappahannock River's left bank; above Gingoteague Creek and east of Port Conway.

Tacopacon Spring (Richmond County Deed Book 1 [1692-1693]:79-80) (1681)

TANKES QUEENS

Creek: New Kent County; a tributary on the Pamunkey River's right side; now called Mill Creek. "Tanks" was the Powhatan Indian word for 'little" or "minor."

Tanx (PB 3:13) (1654)
Tankes Queens (Langston map) (1662)

TANTUCQUACK

Indian Town: Richmond County; on the Rappahannock River's left bank; inside the bend of Little Carter Creek's headwaters.

Tantucquack (Smith map) (1612)

TANX

Creek: Gloucester County; a tributary on the York River's left side; in the immediate vicinity of Porpopotank River; possibly now known as Poropotank Swamp.

Tankes (PB 3:166) (1652)
Tancks (PB 5:248) (1662)

TARRARA

Branch and Creek: Southampton (formerly Isle of Wight) County; a tributary, through Buckhorn Swamp, on the Meherrin River's left bank, running west of Boykins. The name may be Iroquoian rather than Algonquian.

Tarrararah (PB 10:101) (1713)
Tarrahoe (PB 10:149) (1714)
Tarraroe (PB 10:267) (1715)
Tarrara (PB 12:184) (1724)
Tararo (PB 12:265) (1725)
Tarrarro (PB 28:621) (1749)

TASKINAS

Creek: James City County; a tributary on the York River's right side; downstream from Ware Creek.

Taskanosk (PB 5:313) (1662)
Taskoonask (Langston map) (1662)
Taskanas (PB 8:423) (1695)
Taskinask (William Byrd Title Book 203) (1709)
Taskinass (Fry-Jefferson map) (1751)
Teskinas (Anonymous map) (1776)

Powhatan Indian Place Names in Tidewater Virginia

Taskinas (Boye map) (1826)
Taskanask (Bache map) (1857-1858)

TATTOPECKSICK

Field and Spring: King and Queen County; on the Mattaponi River's left side; near the headwaters of Garnetts Creek.

Tattopecksick (PB 4:174) (1658)
Tattapaixsack (PB 5:459) (1663)

TAUXENENT

Indian Town: Fairfax County; on the right side of the Occoquan River, a tributary of the Potomac on its right side, near the Occoquan's widening into Belmont Bay; a king's house.

Tauxesint (Zuniga map, 1608)
Tauxenent (Smith map) (1612)

TEAGUE

Creek: Lancaster County; a tributary on the Rappahannock River's left side; probably modern Midway Creek.

Teagues (Jefferson-Brooke map) (1747)
Teague (Fry-Jefferson map) (1751)

TERACOSIC

Indian Town: City of Suffolk (formerly Norfolk County); on the Nansemond River's left bank, near Elephant Fork.

Teracosic (Smith map) (1612)

TOE INK

Swamp: Charles City County; a tributary on the Chickahominy River's right side.

Toweywinch (PB 4:468) (1660)
Toweywick (PB 4:478) (1661)
Weywick (PB 4:478) (1661)
Towyent (PB 5:278) (1663)
Towwink (PB 7:232) (1683)
Toe Ink (USGS Charles City quadrangle) (1918)

TOMACORECON

Swamp: King and Queen County; a tributary on the Mattaponi River's left side at Walkerton; now known as Walkerton Branch.

Tomacorecon (PB 5:139) (1663)
Tomonocorocon (PB 6:160) (1667)
Tomacoracon (PB 6:515) (1673)
Tomocoricon (PB 6:503) (1674)
Tomocoricond (PB 7:65) (1674)
Tomatacon (PB 7:327) (1683)
Tommacorican (PB 7:624) (1687)
Tomocorocon (PB 9:687) (1705)

TOMAHUND

Creek: Charles City County; a tributary on the Chickahominy River's right bank, upstream from its junction with the James River.

Thomaham (PB 2:171) (1648)
Tamahun (PB 3:152) (1652)
Tomahack (PB 4:49) (1656)
Tomahun (PB 5:395) (1664)

Place: Charles City County; on the Chickahominy River's right bank; close to Juring Point and Tomahund Creek.

Tomahunn (PB 3:307) (1654)

Powhatan Indian Place Names in Tidewater Virginia

TOMAHATTON

Swamp: Prince George County; near the head of Powells Creek, a tributary on the James River's right side.

Tomahatton (PB 14:437) (1732)
Tomaheton (PB 14:492) (1732)
Tommahitton (PB 15:12) (1733)
Tommaheton (PB 15:35) (1733)
Tommohitton (PB 15:183) (1734)

TONYHAM

Branch and Swamp: Charles City County; a tributary on the Chickahominy River's right side; above Cypress Bank Landing and Mattahunk Neck.

Toorihams (PB 4:256) (1658)
Tonyham (USGS Charles City quadrangle) (1917)

Place: Charles City County; on the Chickahominy River's right bank; above Cypress Bank Landing and Mattahunk Neck.

Toriham (Charles City County Court Orders 1737-1751:451) (1747)

TOQUOHUNTA

Swamp: Southampton (formerly Isle of Wight) County; a tributary on the Nottoway River' right side; between Buckland Swamp and Cypress Branch; near the Nottoway Indians' land. The name is probably Iroquoian rather than Algonquian.

Totoquotnunta (PB 10:81) (1713)
Toquothunta (PB 12:196) (1724)
Toquothunta (PB 12:264) (1725)
Toquohunta (PB 15:156) (1734)

Tockwathunty (PB 18:606) (1740)
Tockwothunty (PB 22:123) (1744)
Totoquotunnta (PB 38:734) (1769)
Toquothonta (PB 40:477) (1771)

TOTOPOTOMOY

Creek and Swamp: Gloucester County; a tributary on the right side of the Poropotank River, which is a tributary on the York River's left side; now known as Poplar Springs Branch.

Attopotomoyes (PB 2:359) (1651)
Atapotomoyes (PB 3:128) (1652)
Atapotamoies (PB 3:194) (1652)
Atapotamoyes (PB 4:64) (1652)
Atapotomays (PB 3:16) (1653)
Totopotomoyes (PB 5:355) (1654)
Attapotomays (PB 3:341) (1655)
Attapotamoy (PB 4:534) (1661)
Tottopottomoyes (PB 5:174) (1664)
Totapatomie (PB 7:115) 1681)
Tottapottamoys (PB 7:405) (1684)
Totopotomy (PB 8:314) (1693)
Tattopotomoys (PB 9:178) (1698)
Atapotamoyes (PB 11:59) (1720)

Creek: Hanover County; a tributary on the Pamunkey River's right side; upstream from the U.S. 360 bridge.

Manskind Creek (Langston map) (1662)
Tattapottomoyes (PB 4:284) (1662)
Tottopottomoyes (PB 6:303) (1664)
Tobtopultamoyes (PB 6:303) (1670)
Totopotomy (Herrman map) (1670)
Totopomoyes (PB 6:108) (1672)
Totopotomows (PB 7:5) (1679)
Totopotamoys (PB 7:658) (1688
Totopotomoy (Fry-Jefferson map) (1751)
Tottopotomoy (Anonymous map) (1878)

Powhatan Indian Place Names in Tidewater Virginia

TOTUSKEY

Creek: Richmond County; a tributary on the Rappahannock River's left side; downstream from Accaceek Point.

Toteske (PB 3:174) (1652)
Totaskey (PB 3:58) (1653)
Totoskies (PB 4:154) (1657)
Totoskey (PB 4:160) (1657)
Totoskin (PB 4:260) (1658)
Totoske (PB 5:335) (1662)
Totascay (PB 4:106) (1664)
Todosky (Herrman map, 1670)
Totuscay (Northumberland County Record Book 1670-1672:199) (1671)
Totaskay (Old Rappahannock County Deeds and Wills 1677-1682:364) (1682)
Totaskey (Jefferson-Brooke map) (1747)
Totus Key (Fry-Jefferson map) (1751)
Tutuskey (Henry map) (1770)

Indian Town: Richmond County; on the Rappahannock River's left bank, inland and west of Totuskey Creek.

Totoskey (Old Rappahannock County, Deeds 3:356) (1667)
Totas Chees (HEN II:275) (1669)
Totteros (SPOT I:167) (1712)
Totosha or Tanks Rappahannock Town (MEADE II:478) (1857)

TSENACOMICO

Place: Powhatan Indian name for eastern Virginia.

Tsenacommacoh (HAILE 598) (1612)

TUCKA COMMONS

Marsh and Run: King William County; on the Pamunkey River's left side; now called Sweet Hall Marsh.

Tococomans (PB 4:145) (1657)
Tucka Commons (PB 11:230) (1723)

TUCKAHOE

Creek and Swamp: Northumberland County; a main headwater of the Coan River, itself a tributary on the Potomac River's right side.

Tuckahow (PB 5:326) (1664)
Tuckahoe (PB 5:511) 1664)

TUCKQUAKO

Swamp: Stafford County; on the Rappahannock River's right side; near the falls.

Tuckquako (PB 6:561) (1675)

TUSSUCKEY

Branch: King and Queen County; on the Mattaponi River's left side; at the head of the nameless stream just east of Locust Grove.

Tussuckey (PB 7:121) (1682)

UTENSTANK

Indian Town: King and Queen County; on the Mattaponi River's left bank; just above the mouth of Georges Swamp and opposite Roanes Landing.

Utcustank (Velasco map) (1610)
Utenstank (Smith map) (1612)

UTTAMARKE

Creek: Mathews County; a tributary on

Powhatan Indian Place Names in Tidewater Virginia

the Piankatank River's right side; now known as Dancing Creek, a small stream below Ferry Creek.

Uttamarke (Pindavako [or Pindeabank], Agreement with Edward Wyatt) (1655)

UTTAMUSAK

Indian Town: King William County; on the Pamunkey River's left bank; a site between two small, nameless streams just east of Sweet Hall Landing; a king's house.

Uttamusak (Smith map) (1612)
Uttamussack (CJS I:169) (1612)

UTTAMUSSAMACOMA

Indian Town: Westmoreland County; on the Potomac River's right bank; east of Nomini Creek and near Whiteoak Point.

Uttamussamacoma (Smith map) (1612)

VINCOPO

Creek: York County; a tributary on the York River's right side; two miles northwest of Queens Creek.
Vincopo (PB 1:562) (1638).

WACHAPREAGUE

Indian Town: Accomack County; on the seaside, close to the Wachapreague Channel.

Wachapreague (Northampton County Deeds, Wills, etc. 1657-1666:35) (1654)

Place: Accomack County; on the seaside, close to the Wachapreague Channel.

Wachateege (Northampton County, Deeds, Wills and Orders 3: 217) (1650)
Wachapreague (Northampton County Deeds, Wills, Etc. 1657-1666:7) (1657)
Wattchepreag (PB 4:287) (1659)
Watcheprege (PB 4:104) (1663)
Machapreage (PB 6:372) 1664)
Matchaprege (Accomack County, Deeds and Wills 1663-1666:74) (1664)
Watchapreag (PB 6:80) (1667)
Matsapreack (Herrman map) (1670)
Matchaprig (Northampton County Wills, Deeds, etc. 1711-1718:56) (1713)
Matchepreig (Northampton County Wills, Deeds, etc. 1711-1718:56) (1713)
Matsapreak (Fry-Jefferson map) (1751)
Watchapreak (Marzone map) (1855)

WACONIASK

Indian Town: King George County; on the Rappahannock River's left bank; west of Cleve and downstream from the mouth of Jones Top Creek.

Waconiask (Smith map) (1612)

WAHRANI

Branch, Creek, and Swamp: New Kent and James City Counties; tributaries on the left side of Diascund Creek, itself a tributary on the Chickahominy River's left side.

Warrany (PB 1:534) (1638)
Warranye (PB 1:640) (1639)

Powhatan Indian Place Names in Tidewater Virginia

Waraney (PB 3:89) (1653)
Warreny (PB 3:359) (1655)
Warriny (PB 5:197) (1662)
Wareny (PB 5:359) (1663)
Warrani (PB 6:18) (1666)
Onanye (Herrman map) (1670)
Warini Swamp (USGS Toano quadrangle) (1917)

Fields and Path: James City County; in the immediate vicinity of Diascund Creek.

Warreny (PB 3:388) (1655)
Wareny (PB 4:10) (1655)
Warrany (PB 4:212) (1658)

Indian Town: James City County; on the left bank of Diascund Creek, a tributary on the Chickahominy River's left side.

Warranye (PB 2:62) (1646)
Old Warrany (PB 2:141) (1648)
Old Warraney (PB 4:448) (1660)

Place: James City County; on the Chickahominy River's left bank and also Diascund Creek's left bank, probably close to the creek's mouth.

Warrany Old Landing Place (PB 1:379) (1636)
Warreny (PB 3:387) (1655)

WAQUA

Creek: Brunswick (formerly Prince George) County; on the Nottoway River's right bank; south of McKenney. The name may be Iroquoian rather than Algonquian.

Waquiyough Creek (PB 11:40) (1720)
Waqua Creek (PB 12:533) (1726)

WARIKECK

Indian Town: Southampton County; located on the right side of the Nottoway River, downstream from Raccoon Swamp and upstream from Courtland; a native community that may have belonged to the Weyanocks or the Pochick Nansemonds in the 1660s.

Woriecake Old Fields (WINFREE 44) (1705)
Wariecake (Stanard, "Indians of Southern Virginia," 342) (1707)
Warnkeck (Stanard, "Indians of Southern Virginia," 350) (1707)
Wariekeck (Stanard, "Indians of Southern Virginia," 351) (1707)
Wari-Keck (Stanard, "Indians of Southern Virginia," 351) (1707)
Wareekeck (Stanard, "Indians of Southern Virginia," [conclusion], 8) (1710)

WARRANUNCOCK

Island: King William County; located in the Pamunkey River; below the mouth of Monquin Creek; now known as The Island.

Warrannucock (PB 2:194) (1649)
Warranuncock (PB 2:207) (1649)

Path: King William County; a trail that led from the southeastern part of Pamunkey Neck toward the island of the same name.

Warrannucock (PB 3:291) (1653)

WARRASKOYACK

Bay: Isle of Wight County; on the

Powhatan Indian Place Names in Tidewater Virginia

James River's right side; now known as Burwell Bay.

Weroscoick (Haile 434-435) (1610)
Warrestogack (VCR III:227) (1619)
Warresquioake (PB 1:310) (1635)
Warrasquiake (PB 1:911) (1643)
Waricxqueke (Herrman map) (1670)
Waresquiock (PB 7:417) (1684)
Warresquea (Fry-Jefferson map) (1751)
Warrasqueak (Anonymous map) (1776)
Burrels (Boye map) (1826)

County: one of the original shires or counties established in 1634; renamed Isle of Wight County in 1636.

Warrosquyoake (MCGC 200) (1632)
Warrasquioake (PB 1:185) (1635)
Warresquioake (PB 1:191) (1635)
Warricksqueick (PB 1:333) (1635)
Warwicksquioake (PB 1:346) (1636)
Warrisquick (PB 1:354) (1636)
Warrisquicke (PB 1:354) (1636)
Warwicksquieck (PB 1:400) (1636)
Warwicksquicke (PB 1:402) (1636)
Warwickquick (PB 1:407) (1636)

Creek or River: Isle of Wight County; on the James River's right side; now known as the Pagan River.

Warwicksqeicke (PB 1:67) (1628)
Warwicksqueake (PB 1:68) (1628)
Warresquioake (PB 1:207) (1635)
Warrasquioake (PB 1:233) (1635)
Warresqueick (PB 1:346) (1636)
Warrisquick (PB 1:354) (1636)
Warwickquick (PB 1:407) (1636)
Warwicksquicke (PB 1:408) (1636)
Warwicksquike (PB 1:410) (1636)
Warresquicke (PB 1:613) (1638)
Warresquike (PB 1:634) (1638)
Warrasquiack (PB 2:71) (1646)
Warrisquock (PB 5:174) (1663)

Indian Town: Isle of Wight County; on the left bank of Jones Creek, a tributary of the Pagan River, itself a tributary on the James River's right side; east of Smithfield; a king's house. In 1610, the chief was named Tackonekintaco; his son was named Tangoit (HAILE 622).

Oriskayak (Tyndall map) (1608)
Waraskoyack (CJS I:37) (1608)
Warraskoyack (CJS I:63) (1608)
Warascoyack (Velasco map) (1610)
Warraskorack (Smith map) (1612)
Warraskoyac (CJS II:146) (1612)
Weraskoyk (CJS II:211) (1612)
Weraskoyack (CJS II:229) (1612)
Warrascoyack (HAILE 624) (1612)
Warraskoyock (HAILE 625) (1612)
Wariscoyans (Percy, "A Trewe Relacyon," 273) (1612)
Warescoyke (VCR IV:9) (1623)
Warosquoyacke (HEN I:141) (1629)
Warrosquyoake (MCGC 200) (1632)
Warwicksqeicke (PB 1:127) (1633)
Warresquioake (PB 1:308) (1635)
Warwicksquike (PB 1:410) (1636)
Waraskorack (Vingboons map) (1639)
Marresquicke (PB 1:855) (1642)
Warrisqueak (Ferrar MS 1216) (1653)
Warwicksqueeke (PB 1:126) (1663)
Warrisquick (PB 6:69) (1667)
Warraskorack (Ogilby map) (1676)

Indian Town: King George County; on the Rappahannock River's left bank, at Gingoteague Creek's mouth on the downstream side.

Warisqucock (PB 4:10) (1655)
Warisquock (PB 5:194) (1664)
Warasquit (Richmond County Records 1692-1704:59) (1694)

Parish: Isle of Wight County; formed by 1629; became extinct in 1643 when

Powhatan Indian Place Names in Tidewater Virginia

Isle of Wight County's Upper and Lower Parishes were formed (DSVA 147-148).

Path: Westmoreland County; a trail possibly running from Warisquock Indian Town to the Appomattox Indian Town on Mattox Creek.

Warwicksquick (PB 5:290) (1662)
Warisquick (Westmoreland County, Deeds and Wills 1:226) (1663)
Wariscreeke (PB 5:168) (1664)

WARRAOCEA

Branch: Dinwiddie (formerly Prince George) County; on the left bank of Rowanty Swamp, a tributary of Rowanty Creek and ultimately the Nottoway River on its left side. The name could be either Algonquian or Iroquoian.

Warraocea (PB 20:74) (1741)
Warrohocco (PB 31:618) (1755)

WARREAK

Branch and Field: Southampton (formerly Isle of Wight) County; on the Blackwater River's right side.

Warreak Branch (PB 9:332) (1701)
Wareek (PB 12:453) (1725)

WASHASATIACK

Indian Town: King William County; on the Pamunkey River's left bank; above the mouth of Mehixon Creek.
Washasatiack (Zuniga map) (1608)

WASSANASSON

Branch: Essex County; at the head of Occupacia Creek, a tributary on the Rappahannock River's right side; possibly a branch of modern Black Water Swamp.

Wassanasson (PB 3:351) (1655)
Wassananson (PB 5:327) (1663)
Wassoany (PB 9:596) (1704)

WECUPPOM

Indian Town: Richmond County; on the Rappahannock River's left bank; atop Fones Cliffs, below Brockenborough Creek.

Wecuppom (Smith map) (1612)
Mecuppom (CJS III:174) (1624)

WECKENOSKEEKECKE

Swamp: James City County; on the Chickahominy River's left side; in the vicinity of Crump Swamp.

Weckenoskeekecke (PB 4:52) (1656)

WEEQUIONEDIKE

Branch: King George County; a tributary on the Rappahannock River's left side; probably near the Nanzattico Indians' town (q.v.).

Weequionedike (PB 5:536) (1665)

WERAWAHON

Indian Town: James City County; on the Chickahominy River's left bank; at the mouth of Diascund Creek; in the immediate vicinity of Turner Neck.

Werawahan (Zuniga map) (1608)
Werawahone (CJS I:41) (1608)
Werawahon (Smith map) (1612)

104

Powhatan Indian Place Names in Tidewater Virginia

WEROWOCOMOCO

Indian Town: Gloucester County; on the York River's left bank; at Purtan Bay; a king's house. The name probably means "the chief's (*werowance*) place (*comico*)."

Poetan (Tyndall map) (1608)
Warawcom (Zuniga map) (1608)
Werawocomoco (CJS I:53) (1608)
Werowocomoco (CJS I:53) (1608)
Weracomoco (CJS I:79) (1608)
Weramocomoco (CJS I:61) (1608)
Weramocomoca (CJS I:63) (1608)
Worowcomaco (HAILE 554) (1611)
Werowocomoco (Velasco map) (1610)
Weronocomoco (CJS III:150) (1624)

WERONAUGH

Branch: Essex and King and Queen Counties; in the vicinity of Mattopanny Creek (q.v.) and the head of Piscataway Creek.

Weronaugh (PB 9:214) (1699)

WEYANOCK

Indian Town: Charles City County; on the James River's left bank, on the large triangular-shaped peninsula between Queens Creek and the eastern end of Eppes Island. In ca. 1610, the tribe was ruled by Kaquothocun (HAILE 622); in 1649, their chief was Ascowmett (PP 91, 108).

Winauk (HAILE 114) (1607)
Wynauk (HAILE 117) (1607)
Winocke (VCR III:17) (1609)
Weanoc (Smith map) (1612)
Weanocke (CJS II:242) (1612)
Wyanokes (VCR IV:9) (1623)
Weanoke (MCGC 116) (1626)
Weianoacks (MCGC 151) (1627)
Great Weynoake (PB 1:602) (1630)
Weyenoake (PB 1:295) (1635)
Weyanoake (PB 1:296) (1635)
Weyonoake (PB 1:395) (1636)
Weanock (Vingboons map) (1639)
Weynoke (PB 2:175) (1649)
Weyonoke (PB 2:266) (1650)
Wionoke (PB 2:266) (1650)
Weynock (PB 5:434) (1665)
Weyanock (PB 6:112) (1668)
Wynoak (PB 7:656) (1688)

Indian Town: Prince George County; on the James River's right bank; on the Flowerdew Hundred peninsula. In ca. 1610, a petty chief named Ohoroquoh ruled this town (HAILE 622).

Weanock (Zuniga map) (1608)
Wynogh (Tyndall map) (1608)
Winocke (VCR III:15) (1609)

Indian Town: Prince George County; on Burchen Swamp, at the head of Powells Creek, a tributary on the James River's right side.

Old Town (PB 1:893) (1643)
Weynoake Old Town (PB 2:248) (1650)
Weyanoke Old Town (Prince George Surveyors Record 1794-1824:149) (1808)

Indian Town: Surry County and later Southampton County; a shifting tribal area from the time the Weyanocks left the James River area in 1646 until they finally settled with the Nottoways, by the 1740s.

Wayanoke (Ferrar Papers 1216) (1653)
King Of Weynocks Old Field (PB 6:44) (1666)

Powhatan Indian Place Names in Tidewater Virginia

Weyenoakes (HEN II:274) (1669)
Waehoake (Surry County Orders 1671-1691:55) (1674)
Waynoake (Surry County, Orders 1671-1691:90) (1675)
Weyonock (HEN III:109) (1693)
Weyonoke (Surry County Orders 1691-1713:83) (1693)
Waonoke (Anonymous 1914: 363) (1702)
Wyanoke (BEV 184) (1704)
Wianoke (Stanard, "Indians of Southern Virginia," [conclusion], 10) (1710)
Wyanoke (Bruce, "Boundary Line Proceedings, 1710," 36) (1710)
Waynoke (Bruce, "Boundary Line Proceedings, 1710," 37) (1710)
Warueake (Bruce, "Boundary Line Proceedings, 1710," 39) (1710)

Parish: Charles City and Prince George Counties; spanned both banks of the James River; formed by 1618 and became extinct in 1721.

Waineoke (PB 6:643) (1678)
Wyanoake (PB 7:101) (1681)
Wyanoke (PB 7:130) (1682)
Wayonoake (PB 7:237) (1683)
Wayanoake (PB 7:246) (1683)
Wayenoake (PB 7:305) (1683)
Weyonoake (PB 7:384) (1684)
Wynoake (PB 7:500) (1686)
Winoak (PB 7:657) (1688)
Wynoak (PB 8:238) (1692)
Weyanoake (PB 8:440) (1695)
Waynoke (PB 9:125) (1697)

Place, Point, and Marsh: Charles City County; on the James River's left bank; site settled by Europeans around 1618.

Winauk (HAILE 114) (1607)
Weanock (CJS I:39) (1608)
Wayonoak (PB 1:951) (1642)
Weyanoke (Captaine map) (1781)

Place: Prince George County; on the James River's right bank; an area in the vicinity of Jordan's Point.

Great Weyanoake (PB 1:467) (1637)

Run and Swamp: New Kent County; on the Pamunkey River's right; probably a tributary of Cattail Swamp.

Tanx Weynoake (PB 4:54) (1656)
Wanieoake (PB 4:324) (1662)
Warrieoake (PB 4:324) (1662)
Weyanoke (PB 5:240) (1664)
Wionoke (PB 6:412) (1672)

WHIPPONOCK

Creek: Dinwiddie (formerly Chesterfield) County; a tributary on the Appomattox River's right side; now flows into dammed-up Lake Chesdin. (Name may not be Algonquian.)

WHITSAPENNY

Creek: Accomack County; a tributary on the left side of Pungoteague Creek, itself a tributary of the Chesapeake Bay; probably Warehouse Creek.
Whitsapenny (PB 3:12) (1654)
White Sapenny (PB 4:315) (1661)

WICCAQUNCK

Point: Caroline County; on the Rappahannock River's right bank, above Goldenvale Creek; close to Gouldman Pond.

Wiccaqunck (Old Rappahannock County, Deeds 2: 57) (1658)

Powhatan Indian Place Names in Tidewater Virginia

Quiruck (PB 6:7) (1666)
Wiccoqunck (PB 9:193) (1699)

WICCOCOMSON

Place: Accomack County; above Wachapreague; on the seaside.

Wiccocomson (Accomack County Deeds and Wills 1664-1671:86) (1668)

WICKWAS

Bridge: Charles City County; on the Chickahominy River's right bank above Mattahunk Neck; the bridge spanned Wickwas Run, now a nameless stream.

Wickwa (PB 2:329) (1651)

Place: Charles City County; on the Chickahominy River's right bank; near Mattahunk Neck and the Wickwa Bridge.

Wickwa (PB 2:329) (1651)

Run: Charles City County; a tributary on the Chickahominy River's right side; now a nameless stream above Matahunk Neck; location of the Wickwa Bridge.

Muttnate (PB 2:329) (1651)
Muttuate (PB 2:329) (1651)
Wickwaws (PB 4:15) (1655)
Wickwaas (PB 3:389) (1656)
Nickawas (PB 5:332) (1663)

WICOMICO

Ferry and Place: Northumberland County; somewhere along the Great Wicomico River.

Wiccocommecoe (Northampton County Orders, Deeds, Wills &c 1640-1645:15) (1640) Weckochomicha; (Old Rappahannock County Record Book 1656-1662:104) (1658)
Wecomake (Northumberland County Order Book 1652-1665:399) (1664)
Great Wickorhoinocko (Lancaster County Wills 1674-1689:109) (1678)
Weekacomaco (Lancaster County Wills 1690-1709:107) (1701)

Indian Town: Northumberland County; on the left bank of the Little Wicomico River (a tributary of the Chesapeake Bay at the Potomac River's mouth), near its head; a king's house.

Wighcocomoco (Velasco map) (1610)
Wighocomoco (Smith map) (1612)
Wighcocomoco (CJS II:148) (1612)

Indian Town: Northumberland County; between the right bank of Indian Creek and the Eastern Branch of the Corrotoman River. In 1660 the town was ruled by councilors Pewem and Owasesqaw (or Owasoway); in 1669, the tribe's spokesman was a councilor named Oponomoy; in 1696, the chief's name was Taptico, and his son, William Taptico, succeeded him by 1718 (PP 123, 159).

Wecocomako (Northumberland County, Records 1658-1666:142) (1654)
Wicomico (MCGC 506) (1657)
Wiccocomocoe (PB 4:247) (1658)
Wiccocomoco Indian Town (Lancaster County Deeds and Wills 1654-1661:191) (1659)
Wiccocomoco (PB 4:311) (1662)
Wiccocomico Indian Town (Lancaster County Deeds and Wills 1661-1672:318) (1662)

Powhatan Indian Place Names in Tidewater Virginia

Wiccocomico (PB 5:209) (1663)
Wiccomoco (PB 6:279) (1669)
Wickacomico (HEN II:275) (1669)
Wecocomico (Northumberland County, Orders 1666-1678: 31) (1669)
Wiccocomaco Northumberland County, Orders 1666-1678: 35) (1669)
Wickocomico (Northumberland County, Orders 1666-1678:40) (1669)

Island: Northumberland County; probably an island in the Great Wicomico River.

Wiccomicoe (Northumberland County Order Book 1652-1665:25) (1653)

Parish: Northumberland County; formed in 1648; renamed in 1664 but was revived as Wicomico.

Great Wiccomicoe Parish (Northumberland County Order Book 1652-1665:25) (1653)

Path: Lancaster and Northumberland Counties; a trail between the Wicomico and Morattico Indian towns; recorded in the vicinity of Indian Creek and the head of the Corrotoman River.

Wicocomoco (PB 3:45) (1653)
Wicocomocoe (PB 4:113) (1657)
Wiccocomico (PB 4:129) (1663)
Wickacomico (PB 6:453) (1673)

River (Great): Northumberland County; a tributary of Ingram Bay and the Chesapeake Bay.

Wiccokomoco (PB 1:882) (1643)
Wiccocomoco (PB 1:882) (1643)
Wicocomoco (PB 2:177) (1649)
Wickocomeco (PB 2:218) (1650)
Wickcocomico (PB 2:279) (1650)
Wickcocamaco (PB 2:281) (1650)
Wicocomico (PB 2:305) (1651)
Wicomico (PB 2:358) (1651)
Wicocomocoe (Northumberland County Wills, Inventories &c. 1652-1658:59) (1651)
Wickocomoco (Northumberland County Wills, Inventories &c. 1652-1658:61) (1652)
Wiccocomico (PB 3:1) (1653)
Wicomocoe (Northumberland County Wills, Inventories &c. 1652-1658:59) (1655)
Wicocomocoe (PB 4:11) (1655)
Wiccocomocoe (PB 4:147) (1657)
Wiccomoco (PB 4:193) (1657)
Wiccomocoe (PB 4:275) (1659)
Wiccomico (PB 4:295) (1661)
Wicocomako (Northumberland County Record Book 1662-1666:147) (1665)
Wickocomicoe (Northumberland County Record Book 1666-1670:107-108) (1669)
Wighcocomo (Herrman map) (1670)
Wicocomico (Henry map) (1770)
Wighcocomoco (Fry-Jefferson map) (1751)

River (Little): Northumberland County; a tributary of the Chesapeake Bay at the Potomac River's mouth; also known as Little Wicomico Creek.

Wickocomoke (PB 2:156) (1649)
Wickacomicoe (PB 2:277) (1650)
Wiccocomico (PB 2:325) (1651)
Wicomico (PB 2:358) (1651)
Weckacomco (PB 3:131) (1652)
Wiccocomocoe (Northumberland County Order Book 1652-1665:25) (1653)
Wickocomocoe (Northumberland County Order Book 1652-1665:60) (1654)
Wiccomoco (PB 3:347) (1655)
Wiccocomocoe (PB 4:216) (1658)

Powhatan Indian Place Names in Tidewater Virginia

Wiccomico (PB 4:293) (1661)
Wecocomako (Northumberland County Record Book 1662-1666:171) (1665)
Wicocomako (Northumberland County Record Book 1666-1670: 34-36) (1667)
Wighcoscomo (Herrman map) (1670)
Wighcocomaco (Anonymous map) (1776)
Wighcocomoco (Fry-Jefferson map) (1751)
Wicocomico (Henry map) (1770)

WIGHSAKAN

Indian Town: Gloucester County; on the York River's left bank; in the vicinity of Fox Creek.

Wighsakan (Zuniga map, 1608)

WINAPARTON

Place: Lancaster County; in the vicinity of Indian Creek and the head of the Corrotoman River.

Wynopicton (Lancaster County Wills 1690-1709:41) (1693)

Swamp: Lancaster County; in the vicinity of Indian Creek and the head of the Corrotoman River.

Winaparton (Lancaster County Order Book 1686-1696:19) (1687)

WINKEPIN

Swamp: King and Queen County; a tributary of Dragon Swamp, which is the headwaters of the Piankatank River.

Winkepin (PB 4:187) (1658)

WINSACK

Indian Town: Richmond County; on the left bank of the Rappahannock River; southeast side of Cat Point Creek's mouth.

Winsack (Smith map) (1612)

WINTERPOCK

Branch, Creek, and Run: Chesterfield County; a tributary on the Appomattox River's left bank; flows through the crossroads of Winterpock and down to near the head of Lake Chesdin; in the vicinity of Eppington Plantation. (The name may not be Algonquian.)

Wintopock (PB 9:540) (1703)
Wontapock Run (PB 10:177) (1714)
Wentopock Branch PB 13:226) (1727)
Wintipock (Fry-Jefferson map) (1751)
Witipomack (Captaine map) (1781)
Winterpock (Wood map) (1820b)

Ford: Chesterfield County; old crossing of Winterpock Creek; on the Appomattox River's left bank; in the vicinity of Eppington Plantation.

Wontopock Ford (PB 10:337) (1717)

Place: Chesterfield (formerly Henrico) County; a grand patent or very large tract of land that enveloped what became Eppington Plantation.

Wortapock (PB 8:153) (1690)
Wontapock (PB 10:177) (1714)
Wintopock (PB 10:301) (1716)
Wintopoc (PB 12:306) (1725)

Powhatan Indian Place Names in Tidewater Virginia

WINTICOMACK

Creek: Amelia (formerly Prince George) County; a tributary on the Appomattox River's right bank; to the west of the crossroads known as Whites Store. (The name may not be Algonquian.)

Winticomaick PB 12:111) (1724)
Winticomack (Bristol Parish Vestry Book 55) (1732)
Wintipomack (Fry-Jefferson map, 1751)

WIPPONOCK

Creek: Dinwiddie County; a tributary on the Appomattox River's right side; downstream from Namozine Creek.

Mawhipponock (PB 10:339) (1717)
Mowwhipponock (PB 11:77) (1721)
Manhipponock (PB 11:124) (1722)
Mawhipponack (PB 12:278) (1725)
Mohipponock (Bristol Parish Vestry Book 25) (1727)
Mohiponock (Bristol Parish Vestry Book 55) (1728)
Whipponock (Boye map) (1826)

WIPSEWASIN

Creek: Stafford and King George Counties; a tributary on the right bank of Potomac Creek, itself a tributary on the right side of the Potomac River; now called Black Swamp Branch, which forms part of the boundary between Stafford and King George Counties.

Wipsewasin (PB 5:432) (1665)
Whiptewasin (PB 5:514) (1666)
Weepsiwasson (PB 6:174) (1668)
Whipsewaughson (HEN 9:244) (1776)
Whippawanson (Braden map) (185[-])
Whippawamsick (Gilmer map) (186[-])

Point: King George County; on the right bank of Black Swamp Branch's mouth.

Whippawanson (Braden map) (185[-])

WISCAPONSON

Creek: Northampton County; a tributary of the Chesapeake Bay; now called The Gulf.

Wiscapanso (PB 1:275) (1635)
Wiscoponson (PB 5:401) (1664)
Whiscoponson (Northampton County, Orders 9:49) (1667)

Place: Northampton County; a place near Wiscaponson Creek or The Gulf.

Wiscaponson (PB 1:499) (1637)

WYANOHKINKE

Indian Towns: Southampton County; on the Blackwater River and elsewhere in the Southside.

Wyanohkinke (Stanard, "Indians of Southern Virginia," [conclusion], 10) (1710)

YEOCOMICO

Creek or River: the boundary between Northumberland and Westmoreland Counties; a tributary on the Potomac River's right side.

Yeokomico (PB 1:926) (1643)
Yokomoco (PB 1:931) (1643)

Powhatan Indian Place Names in Tidewater Virginia

Yokomico (Northumberland County Wills and Inventories 1652-1658:23) (1643)
Yeacomico (PB 2:248) (1650)
Yeococomico (PB 2:322) (1651)
Eusrocomoco (Northumberland County, Deeds and Orders 1650-1652:50) (1651)
Yousromoco (Northumberland County, Deeds and Orders 1650-1652:50) (1651)
Tanx Yeocomico (PB 3:92) (1652)
Yeoacomico (PB 3:126) (1652)
Yeocomocoe (Northumberland County Wills and Inventories 1652-1658:19) (1653)
Yeocomoco (PB 3:38) (1653)
Yoacomacoe (PB 4:40) (1656)
Yoecomocoe (PB 4:132) (1657)
Yeocomocoe (PB 4:162) (1657)
Yocomocoe (PB 4:227) (1658)
Yeoacomoco (Northumberland County Record Book 1658-1662:55) (1660)
Yoacomico (PB 5:175) (1664)
Yoacomake (Northumberland County Record Book 1662-1666:132) (1664)
Yeocomaico (Stafford County Record Book 1686-1693:158a) (1690)
Yeacomako (Northumberland County Record Book 1666-1670: 34) (1667)
Yohocomoco (PB 6:200) (1668)
Yoacomoco (Herrman map) (1670)
Yeocomico (PB 6:68) (1677)
Yoacomaco (Richmond County Deed Book 1693-1695:184) (1691)
Yocomoco (Fry-Jefferson map) (1751)
Yocomoco (Anonymous map) (1776)
Yocomico (Madison map) (1807)

Neck: Northumberland County; on the Yeocomico River's left bank; now called Sandy Point Neck.

Yeocomico (PB 3:15) (1653)
Yeocomocoe (PB 4:135) (1657)

Place: Northumberland County; on the Yeocomico River's left bank, near Cherry Point Neck and the glebe land.

Yoacomicoe: (Northumberland County Order Book 1652-1665:60) (1654)
Yeocomoco (PB 5:348) (1655)
Yeocomocoe (PB 4:141) (1657)
Yoacomako (Northumberland County Record Book 1662-1666:165) (1665)
Yoacomaco (Richmond County Deed Book 2 [1693-1695]:86-87) (1691)

Point: Northumberland County; on the Yeocomico River's left bank; the tip of Sandy Point Neck; now called Lynch Point.

Yeocomoco (PB 3:39) (1652)

YOSOCOCOMOCO

Creek or Run: Prince William County; a tributary on the Potomac River's right side; now called Powells Creek.

Yosococomoco (PB 4:116) (1657)
Yosococomocoe (PB 4:195) (1658)
Yosockcocomocoe (PB 4:210) (1658)
Yosococoemocoe (PB 4:235) (1658)
Yeocomoco (PB 4:305) (1661)
Yeoassacomico (PB 6:617) (1677)
Yeosiocomico (PB 8:618) (1677)

YOUGHTANUND

Indian Town: Hanover County; on the Pamunkey River's right bank, downstream from the mouth of Tottopottomoy Creek; a king's house. In ca. 1610, Pomiscutuck was the chief of this town, which was the capital of Youghtanund territory along both banks of the Pamunkey River (HAILE 628).

Powhatan Indian Place Names in Tidewater Virginia

Youghtamong (BAR I:97) (1607)
Youghtanund (CJS I:51) (1608)
Youghtanand (CJS I:57) (1608)
Youghtanum (CJS I:91) (1608)
Youghtanu (Zuniga map) (1608)
Yaughtawnoone (HAILE 486) (1610)
Yawtanoone (HAILE 485) (1610)
Youghtamond (HAILE 628) (1612)
Youghtamudgh (Vingboons map) (1639)
Youghamond (Farrer map) (1651)

River: boundary between King William, New Kent, and Hanover Counties; named by the Indians after the most prominent town along its length; English-speakers have called it the Pamunkey River after the tribe living along it down to the present.

Youghtanan (CJS I:51) (1608)

INDEX TO INDIAN PLACE NAMES

Accahannock, 68

Accohanock, 68,
   69

Accokeek,
   Creek, 1
   Indian Town, 1
   Place, 1
   Point, 1

Accomack,
   County, 1
   Creek, 1
   Indian Towns, 1
   Parish, 2
   Place, 2

Acconoc, 2
   Indian Town, 2

Accoqueck,
   Indian Town, 2

Accosumwinck,
   Indian Town, 2

Accotink,
   Bay, 2
   Creek, 2

Acoughtank,
   Indian Town, 2

Acquack,
   Indian Town, 2

Acquinton,
   Creek, 2

Swamp, 2
Parish Church, 3

Acquasca,
   Neck, 3

Ahorecock, 8

Ajacan,
   Place, 3

Amacoencock,
   Indian Town, 3

Amburrocomico,
   Branch, 3
   Creek, 3

Anancock, 71

Anaskenoans,
   Indian Town, 3

Anchanachuck,
   Place, 3

Annogotegue, 3

Ante Shuroh, 26

Antepoison, 5

Antommcaseword,
   Creek, 3

Apanaock,
   Indian Town, 3

Apasus,

Indian Town, 3

Apostoquo,
   Creek, 4
   Swamp, 4

Appocant,
   Indian Town, 4

Appomattox,
   Bay, 4
   Creek, 4
   Indian Towns, 4, 5
   Parish, 5
   River, 5

Aquakick,
   Indian Town, 5

Aquatt,
   Place, 5

Aquia,
   Creek, 5
   Indian Town, 6
   Place, 6
   River, 5

Aquintenocco,
   Creek, 6
   Swamp, 6

Aquoconde, 69

Armogotegue,
   Creek, 6

Arokoke,
   Creek, 6

Index to Indian Place Names

Arracaico,
 Branch, 6
 Swamp, 6

Arracock,
 Creek, 7

Arratico,
 Creek, 7

Arrohattock,
 Creek, 7
 Indian Town, 7
 Path, 7
 Place, 7
 Territory, 7

Arsantans,
 Creek, 8
 Meadow, 8
 Swamp, 8

Asasaticon, 64

Asiskewincke, 2

Askakep,
 Indian Town, 8

Askamancock, 8

Askecocack,
 Indian Town, 8

Assamoosick,
 Swamp, 8

Assanamayuscock,
 Branch, 8
 Creek, 8
 Swamp, 8

Assaomeck,
 Indian Town, 9

Assateague,
 Inlet, 9
 Island, 9

Assawoman,
 Creek, 9
 Inlet, 9
 Island, 9
 Place, 9

Assesquin,
 Creek, 9

Assuweska,
 Indian Town, 9

Atapotomoyes, 99

Attopottomoyes, 99

Attamtuck,
 Indian Town, 10

Attamuspincke,
 Indian Town, 10

Attanoughkomouck,
 Place, 10

Attapin,
 Creek, 10

Aubomesk,
 Indian Town, 10

Aureuapeugh,
 Indian Town, 10

Ausaticon, 64

Awhorecock, 8

Bockatenock,
 Bay, 10
 Creek, 10
 Place, 10

Candaungack, 94

Cantaunkack,
 Indian Town, 11

Capahosack,
 Creek, 11

Capahosic,
 Creek, 11
 Indian Town, 11
 Place, 11

Caposepock, 35

Cassapecock,
 Indian Town, 11

Cattachiptico,
 Indian Town, 11

Cattalowman, 24, 25

Cawjick, 26

Cawsunker,
 Swamp, 11

Cawunkack,
 Indian Town, 11

Cawwontoll,
 Indian Town, 11

Cecocomake,
 Indian Town, 12

Index to Indian Place Names

Chacoma,
  River, 12

Chamockin,
  Place, 12
  Swamp, 12

Cappatsowsick, 12

Chappawamsick,
  Creek, 12

Chawopo, 19, 20

Chechobanke,
  Indian Town, 12

Checktanck,
  Creek, 12

Cekakawon, 15, 16

Chekroes,
  Bay, 12
  Branch, 13
  Creek, 13
  Neck, 13

Checopissowo,
  Indian Town, 13

Chepeco,
  Indian Town, 13

Cherako,
  Ferry, 13

Cheriton,
  Creek, 13

Chesakawon,
  Indian Town, 13

Chesapeake,
  Bay, 13
  Creek, 14
  Indian Town, 14
  River, 14

Chesconnessex,
  Creek, 14
  Indian Town, 14
  Place, 15

Chespaiack,
  Path, 15

Chesticond, 13

Chestuxen,
  Creek, 15
  Run, 15

Chetank, 22

Cheteckcaurah,
  Creek, 15
  Swamp, 15

Chonamun,
  Branch, 15

Chicamuxen,
  Place, 15

Chickacone,
  Indian Town, 15
  Parish, 15
  Path, 16
  Place, 16
  River, 16

Chickahominy,
  Forts, 16
  Gate, 16
  Indian Towns, 16, 17

Parish, 17
Ridge, 17
River, 17
Swamp, 17
Tribe, 16

Chickonessex, 14

Chincoteague,
  Bay, 18
  Creek, 18
  Indian Town, 18
  Inlet, 18
  Island, 18

Chingandehee,
  Creek, 18

Chingaskin, 30

Chingateague, 30

Chingogan,
  Place, 19

Chingohan,
  Creek, 19

Chingoskin, 30

Chipeaks,
  Creek, 19

Chippiake,
  Creek, 19

Chippokes,
  Creek (Upper), 19
  Creek (Lower), 19
  Indian Town, 20
  Neck, 20
  Places, 20
  Point, 20

Index to Indian Place Names

Chiskiack,
 Creeks, 20
 Indian Towns,
  20, 21
 Parish, 21
 Path, 21
 Territory, 20

Chohuncock,
 Branch, 21

Chopawamsic,
 Creek, 21

Chosicke
 Indian Town, 21

Chotank,
 Creek, 22
 Indian Town, 22

Chowoman,
 Branch, 22

Chuckatuck,
 Creek, 22
 Place, 22

Chyinak, 95

Cinquack,
 Indian Town,

Cinquaetock,
 Indian Town, 22

Cinquoteck,
 Indian Town, 23

Coan, 15, 16

Cohoke,
 Creek, 23

Marsh, 23
Swamp, 23

Comistanck
 Branch, 23

Comokee, 1

Compekeeke
 Creek, 23

Conecocks
 Brook, 23
 Path, 23
 Swamp, 23

Conjurer's Field,
 Marsh, 23

Conjuring Point,
 Point, 23

Connawoman, 26

Copamco,
 Bay, 23
 Island, 23

Coppahaunk
 Branch, 24
 Indian Town, 24
 Swamp, 24

Corapeake, 72

Coroneesaw,
 Swamp, 24

Corowoman, 26

Corrattawomen,
 Branch, 24
 Creek, 24

Corrotoman,
 Bay, 24
 Creeks, 24
 Indian Towns,
  24, 25
 Place, 25
 Point, 25
 River, 25

Coss Coss,
 Creek, 25

Cossatomen, 24,
 25

Cotchawesco,
 Place, 25

Cotcshuroh,
 Branch, 26

Cotteshoraw,
 Branch, 26

Cousiac,
 Creek, 26
 Marsh, 26

Cowawoman,
 Path, 26

Craddock, 26

Cunicott, 23

Currawaugh,
 Place, 26
 Swamp, 26

Currioman,
 Bay, 26
 Cliffs, 26
 Creek, 26

Index to Indian Place Names

Currituck,
　Creek, 27

Custipa,
　Place, 27

Cuttatawoman, 24, 25

Dancing Point, 27

Diascund,
　Creek, 27
　Place, 27
　Swamp, 27

Dogue,
　Branch, 27
　Creek, 28
　Indian Towns, 28
　Island, 28
　Path, 28
　Run, 28

Eackatonke,
　Place, 29

Ekeks,
　Branch, 29

Ekepace, 71, 72

Enocomoe,
　Place, 29

Episkapanke, 71, 72

Genito,
　Creeks, 29

Gibsey,
　Creek, 29

Gingaskin,
　Indian Town, 29

Gingoteague,
　Branch, 30
　Creek, 30
　Swamp, 30

Harrowattocks, 7

Heartquake,
　Creek, 30
　Swamp, 30

Horecock, 8

Hungars,
　Creek, 30

Hunkepen,
　Point, 30

Husquamps,
　Place, 31

Indian Bridge,
　Places, 31

Indian Branch,
　Branch, 31

Indian Burying
　Ground,
　Place, 31

Indian Cabin,
　Branch, 31
　Necks, 31

Indian Creek,
　Creeks, 31, 32

Indian Field,
　Creek, 32
　Necks, 32
　Path, 32

Indian Ferry,
　Ferry, 32

Indian Fort,
　Place, 32

Indian House Thicket,
　Place, 33

Indian Path,
　Path, 33
　Road, 33

Indian Point,
　Points, 33

Indian Quarter,
　Creek, 33

Indian River,
　River, 33

Indian Snares,
　Brook, 33

Indian Spring,
　Springs, 33, 34
　Swamp, 34

Indian Stone,
　Place, 34

Indian Swamp,
　Swamp, 34

Indian Town,
　Branch, 34
　Communities, 34
　Creeks, 34

Index to Indian Place Names

Island, 35
Neck, 35
Point, 35
Swamp, 35

Indian Weir,
  Place, 35

Johnchecohunk,
  Swamp, 35

Juring Point, 23

Kapawnich,
  Indian Town, 35

Kaposepock,
  Indian Town, 35

Kecoughtan,
  Indian Town, 35
  Parish, 36
  Places, 36
  River, 36

Keeskiah, 20, 21

Kegotank
  Bay, 36
  Creek, 36
  Indian Town, 36
  Place, 36

Kenecock, 23

Kerahocak
  Indian Town, 37

Keseokenseeke,
  Swamp, 37

Kimages,
  Creek, 37

Kimeno, 96

Kingcopsico,
  Point, 37

Kiskiack, 20, 21

Kittawan
  Branch, 37
  Creek, 37

Kupkipcock
  Indian Town, 37

Laichecohanck
  Neck, 37

Macaughtions, 58

Maccosoneck
  Creek, 37

Machacomico,
  Swamp, 38

Machapreague, 101

Machezan,
  Place, 38

Machimedes,
  Creek, 38
  Place, 38
  Swamp, 38

Machipongo,
  Branch, 38
  Creeks, 38
  Indian Towns, 38, 39
  Island, 39
  Neck, 39
  Places, 39

River, 39
Sandbar, 39

Machodoc,
  Creek, Lower, 39
  Creek, Upper, 40
  River, Lower, 39
  River, Upper, 40
  Indian Towns, 40
  Necks, 40, 41
  Parish, 41
  Path, 41
  Place, 41

Machotank,
  Place, 41

Mackatouses
  Creek, 41

Macksoomuck
  Neck, 41

Maddicon, 46

Magothy,
  Bay, 41

Mahixon, 53

Mama Sheement,
  Place, 42

Mamanahunt,
  Indian Town, 42

Mamanassy,
  Indian Town, 42

Managirack,
  Path, 42

Manakin,

Index to Indian Place Names

Creek, 42
Place, 42

Manapacant, 54

Manga Kemoxon
  Indian Town, 42

Mangohick,
  Creek, 43

Mangoraca,
  Indian Town, 43

Mangorick,
  Place, 43

Mangoright,
  Point, 43

Manhipponock, 109

Manimass,
  Creek, 43

Mannahorradons,
  Neck, 43

Manoakin,
  Place, 43
  River, 43

Manosquosick, 54

Manquin,
  Creek, 43
  Swamp, 43

Mansa,
  Indian Town, 44

Manskin
  Fort, 44

Indian Towns, 44
  Place, 44

Manskind, 99

Mansotanzic
  Creek, 44

Mantapike,
  Creek, 44
  Places, 44

Mantapoyok, 63

Mantoughquemec,
  Indian Town, 44

Mantua,
  Ferry, 44

Mapsico,
  Creek, 45
  Place, 45

Maquer, 42

Maracossic,
  Creek, 45
  Swamp, 45

Marracoones,
  Creek, 45

Marraquince, 51

Martoughquaunk,
  Indian Town, 45

Marumsco,
  Creek, 45

Massacoon,
  Creek, 45

Massaponax,
  Creek, 45
  Run, 45
  Swamp, 45

Massawoteck,
  Indian Town, 46

Massinacach,
  Indian Town, 46

Massiponey,
  Creek, 46

Matachepeneck,
  Creek, 46

Matadequin,
  Creeks, 46
  Path, 47
  Run, 47

Matahunk,
  Neck, 47

Matchemapps,
  Branch, 47

Matchocoes, 45

Mathomeedes, 38

Matchopick,
  Indian Town, 47

Matchotank,
  Creek, 47
  Place, 47

Matchut,
  Indian Town, 47

Matchutt,

Index to Indian Place Names

Indian Town, 47

Matchycomicoe,
  Branch, 47
  Place, 48

Mathomauk,
  Indian Town, 48

Matomkins, 55

Matsapreak,
  Creek, 48
  Inlet, 48

Matsihapunck,
  Shoals, 48

Mattacock,
  Creek, 48
  Indian Town, 48
  Swamp, 48

Mattacocy,
  Branch, 48
  Creek, 48

Mattacunt,
  Indian Town, 48

Mattadqun, 46

Mattalunt, 47

Mattanock
  Indian Town, 48

Mattaponi,
  Creeks, 49
  Fort, 49
  Indian Ferry, 49
  Indian
    Reservation, 49

Indian Towns, 49
Indian Tribes, 49
Necks, 50
Path, 50
Places, 50
Rivers, 50, 51
Run, 49

Mattaquince,
  Swamp, 51

Mattasack,
  Creek, 51

Mattasip,
  Neck, 51
  Place, 51

Mattasup,
  Swamp, 51

Mattawambs, 52

Mattawoman,
  Creek, 52
  Indian Town, 52

Mattawompson,
  Creek, 52

Mattehatique,
  Indian Towns, 52

Matterdam, 46

Mattex, 4, 5

Matticoe, 45

Mattoax,
  Place, 52

Mattoones,

Creeks, 52, 53
Indian Town, 53
Sunken Ground, 53

Mattox, 4, 5

Mattum Sarkin,
  Place, 53

Matunsk,
  Indian Town, 53

Maukes, The Great
  Place, 53

May-Umps, 59

Mazapin,
  Swamp, 53

Mazinoaos,
  Indian Town, 53

Mechumps,
  Creek, 53

Mecuppom, 104

Mehixen,
  Branch, 53
  Creeks, 53
  Fort, 54
  Place, 54

Menascosic,
  Indian Town, 54

Menapucunt,
  Indian Town, 54

Menaskunt,
  Indian Town, 54

Index to Indian Place Names

Mencococond, New
  River, 54

Mencughtas,
  Indian Town, 54

Menenask,
  Indian Town, 54

Menmend,
  Creek, 54
  Indian Town, 54

Menokin,
  Bay, 55
  Place, 55
  Run, 55
  Swamp, 55

Messongo,
  Creek, 55

Metomkin,
  Bay, 55
  Branch, 55
  Creeks, Great, 55
  Creek, Little, 55
  Indian Town, 55
  Inlet, 56
  Island, 56
  Place, 56
  Point, 56

Miompses, 27, 28

Mitchamoxen,
  Place, 56

Mobjack,
  Bay, 56
  Path, 56

Mockorn,
  Creek, 56
  Island, 56

Mohipponock, 109

Mohixen, 53

Mokete,
  Indian Town, 57

Momtapweake,
  Place, 57

Monack,
  Neck, 57
  Swamp, 57

Monahassanugh,
  Indian Town, 57

Monacan, 42

Monasukapanough
  Indian Town, 57

Moncusaneck
  Creek, 57
  Place, 57
  Road, 57
  Run, 57
  Swamp, 58

Mondui
  Creek, 58

Moncuin, 43

Monquer, 43

Monzation, 64

Morattico,
  Creek, 58

Indian Town, 58
Path, 58
Point, 59
River, 59

Morinogh,
  Indian Town, 58

Morotsny,
  Branch, 59
  Creek, 59

Mountsack,
  Place, 59

Moyaons
  Indian Town, 59

Moysonec
  Indian Town, 59

Muncusneck, 57

Muquer, 43

Musconte,
  Branch, 59

Muskemino, 96

Musketank,
  Indian Town, 59

Muskiminoughk, 96

Muskunt, 47

Muttamussensack
  Indian Town, 60

Muttnate, 106

Muttnate,

121

Index to Indian Place Names

Run, 60

Muzazin,
  Swamp, 60

Myghtuckpassun,
  Indian Town, 60

Myomps,
  Place, 60

Namassingakent,
  Indian Town, 60

Nameroughquena,
  Indian Town, 60

Namozine,
  Creek, 60
  Ferry, 61
  Road, 61

Nanapoyac, 44

Nandtanghtacund,
  Indian Town, 61

Nandua,
  Creek, 61
  Indian Town, 61

Nansemond,
  Bay, 62
  County, 62
  Creek, 62
  Indian Towns, 62
  Neck, 62
  River, 63

Nanapoyac,
  Indian Town, 63

Nantecock,
  Creek, 63
  Neck, 63

Nantupcoy,
  Neck, 63
  Run, 63

Nantypoyson,
  Creek, 63
  Neck, 64
  Path, 64
  Point, 64

Nanzamoxen,
  Creek, 63

Nanzatico,
  Bay, 64
  Indian Towns, 64
  Path, 64

Nanzenin, 60

Nassawadox,
  Creek, 65
  Indian Town, 65
  Neck, 65
  Place, 66
  River, 65

Natchosiq, 39

Nawacaten,
  Indian Town, 66

Neabsco,
  Creek, 66
  Place, 66

Nechanicok,
  Indian Town, 66

Necotowance,
  Creek, 66
  Path, 67
  Place, 67
  Swamp, 67

Nehuntas,
  Creek, 66

Nepawtacum,
  Indian Town, 67

Nesums,
  Creek, 67

Nicatawance, 23

Niccatiwanse, 23

Nickahooke
  Branch, 67

Nickawampus,
  Creek, 67

Nickawas, 106

Nimcock,
  Creek, 67
  Indian Towns, 68

Niopsco, 66

Nomini,
  Bay, 68
  Creek, 68
  Ferry, 68
  Indian Town, 68
  Parish, 68
  Path, 68
  River, 68

Nonsowhaticond, 61

Index to Indian Place Names

Nundue, 26

Nungeocicoe, 64

Nusaponucks, 45

Oatspakety,
  Creek, 68

Occoconson,
  Place, 68

Occohannock,
  Creek, 69
  Indian Town, 69
  Parish, 69
  Path, 70
  Place, 70

Occoquan,
  Bay, 70
  River, 70

Occaneechi,
  Path, 70
  Swamp, 70

Occupacia,
  Creek, 70

Ochahannauke,
  Indian Town, 71

Ohoreek,
  Swamp, 71

Omoy,
  Creek, 71

Onachymoyes,
  Place, 71

Onancock,
  Creek, 71
  Indian Town, 71
  Place, 71

Opahock,
  Indian Town, 72

Oppactenoke,
  Creek, 72

Opiscatumeck,
  River, 72

Opiscopank,
  Creek, 72
  Indian Town, 72

Oquomock,
  Indian Town, 72

Oquonock or
Oqusnock,
  Indian Town, 72

Oracon,
  Creek, 72

Orapagus,
  Creek, 72

Orapax,
  Indian Town, 72

Orapeak,
  Creek, 73
  Place, 73
  Swamp, 73

Oroccock,
  Branch, 73

Osamkateck,
  Indian Town, 73

Ottachugh, 73
  Indian Town,

Ozaiawomen, 73
  Indian Towns,

Ozenick,
  Indian Town, 73

Pacosomaco,
  Creek, 73

Paemotinck,
  Place, 73

Pamamomeck,
  Indian Town, 73

Pamareke,
  Indian Town, 73

Pampatike,
  Creek, 73
  Ferry Landing, 74
  Place, 74

Pamuncoroy,
  Indian Town, 74

Pamunn,
  Place, 74

Pamunkey,
  Indian Town, 74
  Indian Reservation, 74
  Neck, 75
  Paths, 75
  Place, 75
  River, 75

Papacoone,
  Island, 75

Index to Indian Place Names

Papatacon,
  Creek, 75

Papiscone,
  Indian Town, 75

Paraconos,
  Indian Town, 76

Parraketo,
  Point, 76

Pasatinck,
  Creek, 76
  Run, 76

Pasaughtacock,
  Indian Town, 76

Paspahegh,
  Creek, 76
  Indian Towns, 76
  Place, 77
  Territory, 76

Paspanegh,
  Indian Town, 77

Passapatanzy,
  Creek, 77
  Indian Town, 77
  Place, 78
  Run, 77

Passaunkack,
  Indian Town, 77

Pastcock,
  Creek, 78

Pawcocomocac,
  Indian Town, 78

Peckatowns,
  Place, 78

Pemacrey,
  Neck, 78

Peminoe,
  Creek, 78
  Place, 78

Pepetico,
  Branch, 78
  Creek, 78
  Swamp, 78

Perpertocks,
  Creek, 78

Peumansend,
  Creek, 79
  Run, 79
  Swamp, 79

Photomoke,
  Creek, 79

Piankatank,
  Bay, 79
  Creek, 79
  Ferry, 79
  Indian Town, 79
  Parish, 80
  Place, 80
  River, 80
  Swamp, 80

Pipsco,
  Bay, 80
  Place, 80

Piscataway,
  Creek, 81
  Neck, 81

Place, 81
  Swamp, 81

Pissacoack,
  Indian Town, 81

Pissaseck,
  Indian Town, 81

Pochichery,
  Neck, 81

Pochink,
  Place, 82

Pockatamanio,
  Run, 82

Pockashock,
  Branch, 82
  Creek, 82

Pocomoke,
  Bay, 82
  Branch, 82
  Creek, 82
  Place, 82
  River, 82
  Sound, 82

Pohick,
  Bay, 82
  Creek, 82

Pokatink,
  Swamp, 83

Popoeman,
  Creek, 83

Popomar,
  Branch, 83

Index to Indian Place Names

Poquoson,
  Creeks, 83
  Parish, 83
  Places, 83
  Pond, 83
  Rivers, 83
  Swamp, 84

Poropotank,
  Creeks, 84
  Indian Town, 84
  River, 84
  Swamp, 84

Portobago,
  Bay, 84
  Creek, 84
  Indian Town, 85
  Path, 85
  Swamp, 84

Potank,
  Creek, 85

Potauncac,
  Indian Town, 85

Potnick
  Creek, 85

Potoback,
  Place, 85

Potomac,
  Creek, 85
  Indian Town, 85
  Path, 86
  River, 86

Pottacocock,
  Place, 86

Powakei,
  Swamp, 86

Powcomonet,
  Indian Town, 87

Powetridge,
  Creek, 87

Powhatan,
  Bay, 87
  Branch, 87
  Bridge, 87
  Creek, 87
  Indian Town, 87
  Path, 87
  Places, 87
  Pond, 87
  River, 88
  Swamp, 87
  Tree, 88

Powhite,
  Creeks, 88
  Indian Town, 88
  Path, 88
  Swamps, 88

Poyektank,
  Indian Town, 88

Poykemkack,
  Indian Town, 88

Pungoteague,
  Branch, 88
  Creek, 88
  Indian Town, 89
  Place, 89
  River, 88

Putanak,
  Creek, 89

Quackcohowaon,
  Indian Town, 89

Quantico,
  Creek, 89

Queens,
  Creeks, 89

Queens Grave,
  Creek, 89

Quiacomack,
  Neck, 89

Quichecohanek,
  Place, 90

Quietjanjeck,
  Place, 90

Quioccasin,
  Creek, 90
  Place, 90
  Point, 90

Quioksa,
  Branch, 90

Quirank,
  Place, 90

Quioxters,
  Branch, 90

Quiruck,
  Point, 90

Quiyoughcohannock,
  Indian Town, 90

Quosaugh,
  Indian Town, 91

Index to Indian Place Names

Ramagstuck,
  Place, 91

Rappahannock,
  Bay, 91
  Creeks, 91
  Indian Town, 91
  Marsh, 91
  Path, 92
  Place, 92
  Point, 92
  River, 92

Raptestank,
  Place, 92

Raqueto,
  Branch, 92

Rassawek,
  Indian Town, 92

Rhotanoke,
  Neck, 93

Rickahock,
  Creek, 93
  Indian Towns, 93
  Path, 93
  Places, 93, 94

Rickenaw,
  Creek, 94

Roatank,
  Creek, 94

Rohowick,
  Creek, 94
  Place, 94
  Run, 94
  Swamp, 94

Romancoke,
  Place, 94

Rowanty,
  Creek, 94
  Swamp, 94

Sappony,
  Creeks, 95
  Ford, 95
  Indian Town, 95

Schiminoe,
  Creek, 95

Seacock,
  Swamp, 95

Secobeck,
  Indian Town, 95

Shamapint,
  Indian Town, 95

Shoccoe,
  Creek, 96
  Place, 96

Skicoak,
  Indian Town, 96

Skimino,
  Creek, 96
  Place, 96
  Swamp, 96

Sockobeck
  Indian Town, 96

Susquehannah,
  Branch, 96
  Swamp, 96

Swansicutt,
  Creek, 97

Tacopacon,
  Spring, 97

Tankes Queens,
  Creek, 97

Tantucquack,
  Indian Town, 97

Tanx,
  Creek, 97

Tarrara,
  Branch, 97
  Creek, 97

Taskinas,
  Creek, 97

Tattopecksick,
  Field, 98
  Spring, 98

Tauxenent,
  Indian Town, 98

Teague,
  Creek, 98

Teracosic,
  Indian Town, 98

Toe Ink,
  Swamp, 98

Tomacorecon,
  Swamp, 98

Tomahund,

Index to Indian Place Names

Creek, 98
Place, 98

Tomahatton,
  Swamp, 99

Tonyham,
  Branch, 99
  Place, 99
  Swamp, 99

Toquohunta,
  Swamp, 99

Totopotomoy,
  Creeks, 99
  Swamp, 99

Totuskey,
  Creek, 100
  Indian Town, 100

Tsenacomico,
  Place, 100

Tucka Commons,
  Marsh, 100
  Run, 100

Tuckahoe,
  Creek, 100
  Swamp, 100

Tuckquako,
  Swamp, 100

Tussuckey,
  Branch, 100

Utenstank,
  Indian Town, 100

Uttamarke,
  Creek, 100

Uttamusak,
  Indian Town, 100

Uttamussamacoma,
  Indian Town, 101

Vincopo,
  Creek, 101

Wachapreague,
  Indian Town, 101
  Place, 101

Waconiask,
  Indian Town, 101

Wahrani,
  Branch, 101
  Creek, 101
  Fields, 102
  Indian Town, 102
  Path, 102
  Place, 102
  Swamp, 101

Waqua,
  Creek, 102

Warikeck,
  Indian Town, 102

Warranuncock,
  Island, 102
  Path, 102

Warraskoyack,
  Bay, 102
  County, 103
  Creek, 103
  Indian Towns, 103
  Parish, 103

Path, 104
River, 103

Warraocea,
  Branch, 104

Warreak,
  Branch, 104
  Field, 104

Washasatiack,
  Indian Town, 104

Wassanasson,
  Branch, 104

Wecuppom,
  Indian Town, 104

Weckenoskeekecke,
  Swamp, 104

Weequionedike,
  Branch, 104

Werawahon,
  Indian Town, 104

Werowocomoco,
  Indian Town, 105

Weronaugh,
  Branch, 105

Weyanock,
  Indian Towns, 105
  Marsh, 106
  Parish, 106
  Place, 106
  Point, 106
  Run, 106
  Swamp, 106

Index to Indian Place Names

Whipponock,
 Creek, 106

Whitsapenny,
 Creek, 106

Wiccaqunck,
 Point, 106

Wiccocomson,
 Place, 107

Wickwas,
 Bridge, 107
 Place, 107
 Run, 107

Wicomico
 Ferry, 107
 Indian Towns, 107
 Island, 108
 Parish, 108
 Path, 108
 Place, 108
 River, Little, 108
 River, Great, 108

Wighsakan,
 Indian Town, 109

Winkepin,
 Swamp, 109

Winsack,
 Point, 109

Winterpock,
 Branch, 109
 Creek, 109
 Ford, 109
 Place, 109
 Run, 109

Winticomack,
 Creek, 110

Wipponock,
 Creek, 110

Wipsewasin,
 Creek, 110

Winaparton,
 Place, 109
 Swamp, 109

Wiscaponson,
 Creek, 110
 Place, 110

Wyanohkinke,
 Indian Towns, 110

Yeocomico,
 Creek, 110
 Neck, 111
 Place, 111
 Point, 111
 River, 110

Yosococomoco,
 Creek, 111
 Run, 111

Youghtanund
 Indian Town, 111
 River, 112

INDEX TO INDIAN PEOPLE

Accopatough, 91

Ascowmett, 105

Attasquintan, 74

Attossamunek, 76

Casquesough, George, 40

Chopoke, 91

Cockacoeske, 74

Debbedeavon, 69

Ekeeks, 71

Eriopochke, 50

Essenetaugh, 85

Harquip, 17

Iopassus, 77

Japazaws, 77

Kaquothocun, 105

Kekataugh, 74

Keyghaughton, 11

Kiptopeke, 69

Machamap, 58

Machywap, 15

Mennenhcom, 50

Nansuapunck, 95

Necotowance, 74

Nochetrawen, 14

Oholasc, 90

Ohoroquoh, 105

Ononnamo, 11

Opachancone, 54

Opechancanough, 54, 74

Opitchapam, 74

Oponomoy, 107

Opopohcumunk, 13

Opussonoquonuske, 4

Ossikacan, 21

Ottahotin, 20

Ottondeacommoc, 54

Owasesqaw, 107

Owasoway, 107

Owmohowtne, 50

Parahunt, 87

Pattanochus, 85

Pepiscunimah, 80, 91

Peponngeis, 50

Peracuta, 4

Pertatoan, 40

Pewem, 107

Pindavaco, 21, 101

Pindeabank, 21, 101

Pipsco, 80, 91

Pochins, 35

Pomiscutuck, 111

Powhatan, 11, 35, 42, 72, 74, 87, 88, 91

Tackonekintaco, 103

Tangoit, 103

Tapatiaton, 69

Index to Indian People

Taptico, 107

Taptico, William, 107

Tatahcoope, 91

Taweeren, 91

Tottopottomoy, 2, 74

Tupeisens, 50

Uropaack, 71

Wachicopa, 91

Wackawamp, 69

Wahanganoche, 86

Wassatickon, 21

Werowough, 50

Weyamat, 35

Wowinchopunck, 76

www.ingramcontent.com/pod-product-compliance
Lightning Source LLC
Chambersburg PA
CBHW072151160426
43197CB00012B/2344